"Each substance of a grief hath twenty shadows."

William Shakespeare, *King Richard II*, Act II, Scene 2

# FROM THE SHADOW OF JFK

## The Rise of Beatlemania in America

*Aaron Krerowicz*

AK Books

www.AaronKrerowicz.com

# Contents

# Acknowledgments

Thanks to the many editors who reviewed various drafts of this book and made invaluable contributions to the finished product. These include Hal Rives, Andy & JoAnne Mitchell, Candy Leonard; and especially my parents Polly Waara & John Krerowicz, and dear friends Tristan & Sarah Axelrod.

Thanks as well to Wesleyan University's Olin Library, which holds extensive records – including archives of *The New York Times*, *Washington Post, Life, The New Yorker*, and *Time* – which proved invaluable in conducting research from period sources.

Thanks to my wife and love of my life, Natalie Todd, for all of your suggestions with this book in particular and for all your support in general.

# Preface

Until very recently, whenever I read others' writings about connections between John F. Kennedy and the Beatles, I thought there was
something missing. Most authors, whether in support or criticism of the
notion, gloss over any connection in a few sentences, as if it's obvious.

Several authors do go into more detail. Jonathan Gould's 2007
book *Can't Buy Me Love: The Beatles, Britain, and America* describes
Kennedy as "the first American president to have his sensibilities molded
in the crucible of modern mass culture."[1]

Some authors even acknowledge how the Beatles replaced
Kennedy as symbols of youth, anticipating my own conclusions. In his
2006 book *Meet the Beatles: A Cultural History of the Band that Shook
Youth, Gender, and the World*, Steven D. Stark describes how Kennedy's
assassination "helped create a climate that propelled the Beatles' rise ...
by creating a vacuum for another pop superstar (or set of them) to fill. ...
Without Kennedy, the culture was looking for someone else to, as he
might have put it, pick up the torch for a nation now hooked on the
glamour, thrill, and ferment of youth."[2]

In her 2014 book *Beatleness: How the Beatles and Their Fans
Remade the World*, Candy Leonard, the first author to offer a sociocul-
tural analysis of the entire phenomenon, sets the stage with what she
calls a "brief Beatlecentric and youthcentric look" at the Kennedy era.
She observes that, "like Kennedy, the Beatles were youthful, cool, com-
petent citizens of the world with authentic charisma and a natural ability
to speak off the cuff and charm a crowd. They seemed to represent the
future in the same way Kennedy once had".[3]

It makes sense why books with the massive scope of *Can't Buy
Me Love*, *Meet the Beatles*, and *Beatleness*, (all are over 300 pages and
cover more or less the band's entire career) wouldn't go into great detail
on Kennedy because he is at most a secondary character, entirely outside
of the primary focus on the Beatles. Such depth and consideration of a

---

1    Gould, p. 206
2    Stark, p. 32
3    Leonard, p. 2, 55

person not directly related to the overall theme of the book would be gratuitous. That's why I felt that a book dedicated solely to the comparison was needed to help contextualize and explain what is indeed a compelling relationship.

Perhaps my skepticism was the result of my own youth, having been born well after Kennedy and the Beatles were at their peaks. Maybe had I lived through it, I would have already understood the appeal of both president and band to the youth of the era and culture as a whole. Only upon researching Kennedy for myself did I come to understand just how deep his connection to the Beatles actually is. Since I couldn't find a book that went into the depth I felt the subject demanded, I wrote my own to look exclusively and exhaustively at this one, specific aspect of the band's success.

My goal with *From the Shadow of JFK* is not to replace the other books out there that discuss Kennedy and the Beatles, but rather to provide a more in-depth look at the Kennedy piece of the equation; to more fully 'show the work' behind the conclusions and establish a more complete, well-rounded understanding of Beatles history.

Aaron Krerowicz
Hartford, CT
2 June 2015

# INTRODUCTION

## The Beatles in America in 1963

Beatlemania doesn't have a birth date – it was a gradual progression through the early 1960s as the Beatles gained more and more media coverage, played in increasingly larger venues, and performed for progressively more manic audiences. But Beatlemania does have a birth place: England. By the end of 1963 in Britain, the band's performances could barely be heard over the screams of female fans. The United States, however, remained tepid until the early months of 1964.

The Beatles' success in both countries was a direct result of their commercial recordings. Brian Epstein, the Beatles' manager, signed a recording contract for the band with the British company Electrical and Musical Industries, Ltd. (EMI) on 9 May 1962.[4] It was a deal that would make the Beatles famous and EMI wealthy, for the band would go on to score 17 #1 hits in the British periodical *Record Retailer* between 1963-1969.

Emboldened by the success of the Beatles in England and eager for additional profit, EMI repeatedly requested throughout 1963 that their American counterpart, Capitol Records, distribute the band's music in the United States. Deciding which records to release ultimately fell to Capitol Records' president, Alan Livingston; however, Livingston passed this responsibility on to a trusted associate. In his own words:

> Out of courtesy, 'cause we had no obligation, I would occasionally take an EMI record, English in particular, and release it in the United States with no success whatsoever. There was just no interest in English artists … We had no success at all, but because of the relationship, I felt we had to screen everything they sent us. I couldn't just brush it off, so I gave one of my producers at Capitol the assignment of listening to every EMI record that was sent to us. His name was Dave Dexter.[5]

---

4    Lewisohn 2013, p. 624
5    Spizer, p. 9

A hardcore jazz fan, Dave Dexter despised American Rock 'n' Roll and regarded English popular music with even more disdain. In a 1956 letter, Dexter wrote to EMI:

> We are in a most discouraging revolution in the pop singles field. A great majority of singles are bought not by college students but by mere children, youngsters as young as 11, 12, and 13 years old. They buy strictly for the beat and, as you can tell from the recent Elvis Presley and Guy Mitchell releases over here, the lyrics are juvenile and maddeningly repetitive.[6]

This same man, seven years later, would pass up the opportunity to release Beatles records in the United States on four occasions.[7]

In Dexter's defense, few English recording artists had ever succeeded in the United States to that point. As Epstein described, "The view was that whatever the British did at their best, an American at his best would do very much better."[8] And nobody – Dave Dexter included – had any reason to believe that trend would change any time soon.

With Capitol disinterested, EMI instead granted vending rights to Vee Jay Records, a predominantly black, Chicago-based label. Vee Jay had scored recent successes with Gene Chandler's 'Duke of Earl' and The Four Seasons' 'Sherry', 'Big Girls Don't Cry', and 'Walk Like a Man'. On 7 February 1963, one year to the day before the band made their arrival on U.S. soil, Vee Jay released the first Beatles record in America: the single 'Please Please Me'/'Ask Me Why'.[9] It flopped, selling roughly 5,650 copies by the end of 1963 and failing to make any of the charts.[10]

Given the Beatles' extreme popularity in England, however, they tried again. On 6 May 1963, Vee Jay released the second American Beatles single: 'From Me To You'/'Thank You Girl'.[9] This release fared only marginally better, selling 12,675 copies by the end of September, and peaking on the August *Bubbling Under The Hot 100* chart at number 116.[11] While a definite commercial improvement over the first release, the record's sales paled in comparison to both songs' #1 status in the U.K.

Louise Caldwell, George Harrison's sister (at the time a resident of Illinois), suspected Vee Jay was not adequately promoting her

---

6    Martland, p. 234
7    Spizer, p. 72
8    Epstein, p. 12
9    Spizer, p. 232
10   Spizer, p. 16
11   Spizer, p. 31

brother's band's music, and said so in a letter (apparently lost) to Brian Epstein. In a 23 August response, Epstein wrote, "I am going into everything you say very carefully. I have already instructed persons concerned to change release of the BEATLES' disc to another label. 'She Loves You' will definitely not go out on Vee Jay."[12]

Since neither Vee Jay release had been particularly successful, and with Epstein encouraging switching labels, EMI approached the Philadelphia-based novelty label Swan Records. On 16 September 1963, Swan released the third American Beatles single: 'She Loves You'/'I'll Get You'.[9] It met the same disappointing fate as the first American Beatles single, failing to appear on any of the national charts.[9]

Realizing that with three failed releases it was 'do or die time' for the Beatles in America, Epstein traveled to New York in November. He wanted, he said, "to find out why the Beatles – who were the biggest thing the British pop world had ever known – hadn't 'happened' in America."[13] During his New York visit, Epstein met with Ed Sullivan to negotiate details on the band's performances on The Ed Sullivan Show, and also met with a journalist from *The New Yorker*. "America is ready for the Beatles," the 28 December issue of the periodical quotes the manager. "When they come, they will hit this country for six", a cricket reference equivalent to baseball's home run.[14]

Epstein's efforts paid off when Capitol Records finally decided to give the Beatles a try. "We knew America would make us or break us as world stars,"[15] said Epstein. And so he insisted to Alan Livingston, "I'm not going to give them to you [Capitol] unless you spend $40,000 to promote their first single."[16] Since he already had signed a contract with EMI, Brian lacked the authority to withhold the Beatles' music from Capitol's release should such a promotional budget be denied. It was a moot point, however, because Livingston agreed anyway – probably because he knew that Vee Jay and Swan's releases had failed in part due to lack of promotion.

Livingston also saw potential in the band that Dave Dexter had missed. Quoting Livingston:

> It was obviously something different. The other British groups were either into their own style of music, which didn't appeal to me for play here in the United States, or they were imitative of the US music and not

---

12   Spizer, p. 45
13   Epstein, p. 11
14   *Time*, 28 December 1963, p. 24
15   Epstein, p. 20
16   Geller, p. 71

too good. Here was a different sound and of course the boys had a different look and had great promotional possibilities in the teenage market.[17]

A Capitol Records press release headline dated 4 December 1963
proclaims, "NEW ENGLISH MADNESS TO SPREAD TO THE U.S.;
BEATLEMANIA WILL BE IMPORTED HERE". It went on to read:

> Beatlemania, the totally unprecedented musical phenomenon that has
> turned England topsy-turvy this past year will spread to the United
> States in 1964. Alan W. Livingston, president of Capitol Records, Inc.,
> announced today that his company has concluded negotiations with
> Electric & Musical Industries (EMI), Ltd., for exclusive U.S. rights to
> recordings by The Beatles, the sole cause of the mania. In making the
> announcement, Livingston said: "With their popularity in England and
> the promotion we're going to put behind them here, I have every reason
> to believe The Beatles will be just as successful in the United States.[18]

The extent to which Livingston believed his own words is un-
clear. But with the benefit of hindsight, he certainly appears prescient.

Livingston was sincere about "the promotion we're going to put
behind them". A 23 December Capitol Records memo describes the marketing plan, which included advertisements in *Billboard* and *Cash Box*,
the production and sales of Beatle wigs, distribution of "The Beatles Are
Coming" buttons, a four-page newspaper "which looks deceptively legit-
imate" with plentiful photos and stories, and moving picture displays of
the band to be set up in record stores.[19] Most important, though, were
the promotional copies of the music, to be distributed to radio disc jock-
eys.[19] "The best promotion is to have it played on the air, so somebody
can hear it," explained Livingston. "If nobody can hear it, to hell with it.
It was very easy at the time to get air play. Particularly for Capitol, who
had a good following. So that was the promotion. ... It was the easiest
promotion I've ever seen."[17]

Livingston's promotional budget was put to good use. A two-
page spread in the 4 January 1964 issue of *Billboard* reads:

> BRITAIN'S "BEATLEMANIA" HAS SPREAD TO AMERICA! On TV:
> Jack Paar Show (Jan. 3, NBC-TV)! Ed Sullivan Show (Feb. 9, Feb. 16,
> CBS-TV)! Already seen on Walter Cronkite News (CBS-TV), Hunt-
> ley-Brinkley News (NBC-TV)! Featured in Time, Life, Newsweek and
> newspapers everywhere! Among record buyers "Beatlemania" has
> proved absolutely contagious. Over 3,000,000 discs already sold in Eng-

---

17  Geller, p. 72
18  Spizer, p. 71
19  Spizer, p. 73

land alone. So be prepared for the kind of sales epidemic that made THE BEATLES the biggest-selling vocal group in British history! CALL YOUR CAPITOL SALES REP. TODAY![20]

Not everyone – indeed, not even the more reputable sources – believed the hype. On the same date as the *Billboard* ad release, *The New York Times* insisted, "It would not seem quite so likely that the accompanying fever known as Beatlemania will also be successfully exported. On this side of the Atlantic it is dated stuff."[21]

Paul McCartney vividly remembers telling Brian Epstein "that we wouldn't go to America unless we were number one."[22] But Brian had already booked American performances through both Ed Sullivan and concert promoter Sid Bernstein prior to the Beatles reaching the top of the U.S. charts. In other words, the band would have traveled to the U.S., played The Ed Sullivan Show, and performed at Carnegie Hall even without a top song. But as it turned out, 'I Want To Hold Your Hand' reached #1 on 1 February 1964, six days before their arrival.[23]

At the time, the Beatles were in France, playing a marathon of concerts (as many as three per day between 16 January and 4 February) at the Olympia Theater in Paris.[24] As Paul recalled in *The Beatles Anthology*:

> One night we arrived back at the hotel from the Olympia when a telegram came through to Brian from Capitol Records of America. He came running in to the room saying, 'Hey, look. You are Number One in America!' ... We all tried to climb onto Big Mal's [6-foot 4-inch Mal Evans, a roadie] back to go round the hotel suite: 'Wey-hey!' And that was it, we didn't come down for a week.[25]

From Paris, the Beatles flew back to England on 5 February, spent a day recovering from their French excursion, and on the morning of 7 February boarded another airplane. Destination: New York City and worldwide fame. "If there was a turning point in their career," said Epstein in hindsight, "a specific date on which the breadth and scope of their future was to be altered, then it was the day their Pan Am jet touched down at Kennedy International in New York to a welcome

20    *Billboard*, 4 January 1964, p. 6-7
21    *The New York Times*, 4 January 1964, p. 47
22    Geller, p. 73
23    Whitburn, p. 835
24    Lewisohn 2006, p. 143
25    Beatles 2000, p. 114

which has seldom been equaled in history."[26]

\*   \*   \*   \*   \*   \*   \*   \*   \*

So, what changed? What was so different in the United States between the inconsequential first American release of a Beatles record by Vee Jay on 7 February 1963 and the band's celebrated arrival in America precisely one year later on 7 February 1964? There are no easy answers, but clearly a combination of multifaceted factors were at play. Many of these elements have been studied, discussed, and documented by other authors and scholars, thus there is little reason to consider them in any substantial depth here. But one component of the rise of Beatlemania in America has not yet been exhausted: the assassination of President John F. Kennedy on 22 November 1963.

On one hand, the connection between Kennedy's demise and the Beatles' ascent has been stated to the point of banality, as abundant examples illustrate:

> [America was] hungry for some light diversion from the aftermath of the Kennedy assassination.[27]

> America fell to [the Beatles] on the morning in Dallas that the Presidential motorcade set off on its route.[28]

> We were carved deeply in November 1963 and needed the joy of the Beatles' art to fill and heal the wound. The feelings of exhilaration and immortality that great art confers were so sorely needed after that brutal proof that life is transient.[29]

> [The Beatles were] lapped up by a nation eager to forget JFK's death.[30]

> The record's joyous energy and invention [referring to 'I Want to Hold Your Hand'] lifted America out of its gloom, following which, high on gratitude, the country cast itself at the Beatles' feet.[31]

> In the depressing aftermath of the murder young Americans looked beyond their country for something new and innocent to cheer them up, and heard a fresh, joyful sound coming from England.[32]

---

26   Beatles 2003, Episode 3
27   Schaffner, p. 23
28   Norman 1996, p. 205
29   Goldsmith, p. 110
30   Jackson, p. 106
31   Ian MacDonald, p. 77
32   Sounes, p. 97

For an antidote to the headlines of those dismal weeks, the American media actively sought out a new story: a story that was frivolous, off-beat, and above all, cheerful. It was in this context that America first learned of that bizarre British epidemic known as Beatlemania.[33]

By January the nation wanted desperately to hear something happy, to find a diversion, some distraction from the morbid tragedy that had intruded into our lives. America needed a tonic. Little would anyone have expected it to be a pop group.[34]

Like a proverbial breath of fresh air, the Fab Four arrived on the scene in February 1964, and a nation in mourning became transfixed by "I Want to Hold Your Hand" and the notion – pleasant relief that it was – of meeting the Beatles.[35]

Even Paul McCartney claims a connection between the president's death and the rise of Beatlemania. "There is a sort of healing thing going on again, and I'm proud to be part of that," said the bassist during his fall 2001 concert tour.[36] With his use of the word 'again', Paul refers to the similarity between his tour following the 9/11 World Trade Center terrorist attacks and the Beatles' first American visit and tour in the aftermath of Kennedy's assassination four decades earlier. "We didn't set out to do that with this tour," he continued, "but we're here at the right time."[36]

The basic logic of this "Kennedy Rebound Theory of Beatlemania", so named and greatly expanded upon by Candy Leonard,[37] seems to be that Kennedy's death made America sad, then the Beatles made America happy again. Despite its prevalence, however, this theory is hardly universally accepted. Other authors have rejected any connection between the president and the band in no uncertain terms:

Most of the tired psychobabble on Beatlemania revolves around the cliché about a nation's pent-up anxiety following this national grief. This assumes that had the Beatles not arrived, many of the same teenage girls would have been found weeping in their rooms over the fallen young hero.[38]

The need for diversion cannot seriously be advanced as a factor in the Beatles' success. ... If a need for diversion lay at the heart of Beatlemania, why have the equally troubled 1970s and 1980s produced noth-

33    Shotton and Schaffner, p. 163
34    Brown and Gaines, p. 109
35    Womack and Davis, p. 2
36    Sounes, p. 511
37    Leonard, p. 18
38    Riley, p. 235

ing like the hysteria that attended the Beatles' early years?[39]

Although Kennedy's assassination may have had some effect on the Beatles' popularity – they offered welcome cheer – it was not a major factor.[40]

The indisputable fact is that credit for the Beatles' incredible U.S. conquest was due to only four people – John, Paul, George, and Ringo.[41]

The connection between the death of President Kennedy and the explosion of Beatlemania in America has been blown out of proportion. ... The main reason I embraced the Beatles is the same reason people do 40 years later – the quality of the music. In all due respect to President Kennedy, his death did not cause me to become a Beatles fan. ... I have yet to find any evidence to support the connection.[42]

And, although it's debatable what he meant, even John Lennon – always Paul McCartney's foil – sang in his 1970 song 'God', "I don't believe in Kennedy."

Nevertheless, there is still much to explore about the Kennedy Rebound Theory of Beatlemania and the striking parallels between the 35th American president and the mop-topped Liverpudlian rockers. The Beatles' rise in the wake of Kennedy's fall goes far beyond the simplistic notion that 'Kennedy's death made America sad, then the Beatles made America happy again.' This book attempts to put the rise of Beatlemania in America into proper context and to illustrate those parallels in three parts: First, a consideration of how and why Youth Culture developed and flourished in the mid-20th Century; second, a detailed explanation of how and why Kennedy's political success was a result of his status as a symbol for Youth Culture; and third, discussion of how and why the Beatles' musical success was a direct result of their status as symbols of Youth Culture. A fourth part will summarize and draw conclusions on how the Beatles replaced Kennedy as leaders of Youth Culture.

---

39  Kozinn, p. 81
40  Leigh, p. 34
41  Pawlowski, p. 175
42  Spizer, p. 64

# PART 1

# The Rise of Youth Culture

Much debate exists about Youth Culture: What is it? How can it be defined? Does it even exist at all? The answers, if extant, lie in the plentiful scholarship on the subject.

Many authors suggest that patterns of behavior common among teenagers (such as choices of clothing, music, and language) help define Youth Culture as independent from adult cultures. Some of these authors insist that Youth Culture consciously rejects the values and choices of adult life as a way of establishing personal autonomy. From this perspective, an adolescent "is 'cut off' from the rest of society, forced inward towards his own age group, made to carry out his whole social life with others his own age ... and maintains only a few threads of connection with the outside adult society."[43]

Other authors propose that Youth Culture is not a rejection of adult values but rather the same values merely surfacing in different forms. From this view, adolescents' "interactions with peers support the values of the parents" and "it is misleading to speak of separate adolescent cultures or of general peer versus parental influence" because peer influence and parental influence are fundamentally the same.[44]

Some authors split the difference, arguing that Youth Culture neither rejects nor embraces adult values precisely because it is based on "nonessential" and "trivial matters like those dealing with clothes, music, sports, and dating," choices which "have little carryover to adult life."[45]

Still others contend that traits often thought of as definitive of Youth Culture are actually more representative of society in general and Western culture as a whole. "Identity crises, generation gaps, and peer pressure may be features of adolescent life in contemporary society," ac-

---

43    Coleman, p. 3
44    Kandel and Lesser, p. 166
45    Fasick, p. 158

knowledged Laurence Steinberg in his 2008 book *Adolescence*, "but their prevalence has more to do with the nature of our society than with the nature of adolescence as a stage in the life cycle."[46] From that perspective, Youth Culture lacks differentiation from other forms of culture and therefore does not actually exist.

Regardless of technical definitions and academic distinctions, throughout history American society has progressively understood and valued the differences between childhood and adulthood. Consequently, the U.S. has increasingly encouraged its youth to be youthful. "It is as if, to every period of history, there corresponded a privileged age and a particular division of human life," observes Philippe Ariès in his book *Centuries of Childhood*. "Youth is the privileged age of the seventeenth century, childhood of the 19th, adolescence of the 20th."[47]

"Children in the colonial period," describes historian Elizabeth H. Pleck, "were seen as beings who should adopt adult behavior and assume adult responsibilities as soon as possible" instead of embracing the unique qualities and characteristics of being young. The American Revolution, rooted in notions of equality among people, helped break constructs of hierarchy on many levels, including familial. In this new American society, instead of seeing young people as 'not yet adults', children warranted their own unique considerations and needs. In tandem with this understanding, goods such as books and toys designed specifically for the developmental needs of children emerged in the mid-1800s.[48]

Not only was childhood afforded more understanding and distinction from adulthood, but society's ideas of motherhood also took on added dimensions. This was part of a larger shift towards defined and differentiated roles for all family members. "Husbands became more preoccupied with business matters, and mothers came to spend an increasing amount of time attending to their children," continues Pleck. "The mother, considered the naturally affectionate parent, became the emotional center of the family. Nothing was more sacred than the bond between mother and child."[48]

As these emotional and familial bonds developed, and as parents' understandings of the unique needs of their children evolved, so did techniques of discipline and motivation. Corporal punishment slowly ceded to more compassionate tactics. "There was a growing consensus," writes Steven Mintz and Susan Kellogg in *Domestic Revolutions: A So-*

---

46   Steinberg, p. xv
47   Ariès, p. 32
48   Foner and Garraty, p. 164-165

*cial History of American Family Life*, "that the object of child rearing was not to break a child's will through intense moral or physical pressure but to shape his or her character."[49] Thus, the general objective of American families shifted from practical economic considerations to emotional ones.

\* \* \* \* \* \* \* \* \*

Legislative acts confirm America's progressive emphasis on youth as a developmental period more objectively than any other type of record. In the early 21st Century, the adolescent years are filled with legal landmarks, ages at which a person becomes responsible enough to partake in certain activities in the eyes of the law. But that was not always so.

Throughout the 19th Century, children were often put to work by families desperate to supplement meager wages; in turn, employers were happy to hire young people for monotonous jobs and equally pleased to pay them less than adult workers. According to Irwin Yellowitz in *The Reader's Companion to American History*, child labor in the early years of the nation "was an integral part of the agricultural and handicraft economy."[50] Children were frequently put to work not only on their own family's farm, but also hired out to other farms that needed additional hands.

With the Industrial Revolution of the early 1800s, at a time when massive immigration contributed to a supply of workers of all ages, children were often sent to work in factories. The strenuous work, horrendous hours, and near-negligible wages eventually prompted a reaction in the form of legal regulations, the first of which, passed in Massachusetts in 1836, mandated that workers 14 years of age and younger must attend school a minimum of three months each year. Six years later, the same state passed legislation capping child labor at 10 hours per day.[51] Through the remainder of the 19th Century, other states followed Massachusetts' lead, but the laws were not regularly enforced and loopholes were frequently exploited.

True reform of child labor, and subsequently the early stirrings of Youth Culture, finally occurred in the early 20th Century. The Nation-

---

49    Mintz and Kellogg, p. 58
50    Foner and Garraty, p. 166
51    https://www.continuetolearn.uiowa.edu/laborctr/child_labor/about/us_history.html, accessed 4 April 2015

al Child Labor Committee, formed in 1904, repeatedly launched campaigns for child labor reform.[52] Congress rewarded the NCLC's efforts with legislation in 1916 and 1918, but the Supreme Court struck down both acts as unconstitutional on the grounds that they violated states' rights. "If Congress can thus regulate matters entrusted to local authorities by prohibition of the movement of commodities in interstate commerce," came the majority explanation, "all freedom of commerce will be at an end, and the power the States over local matters may be eliminated, and thus our system of government be practically destroyed."[53]

Only with the economically traumatic Great Depression did actual reform occur. With popular support from the vast millions of unemployed adults at the time who wanted the extra hours, and with President Franklin Delano Roosevelt pressuring the Supreme Court into submission, the government finally passed the Fair Labor Standards Act of 1938. The new law established federal minimum employment ages and maximum employment hours for workers in manufacturing and mining. In 1949, Congress amended the act, expanding the definition of labor to include agriculture, transportation, communications, and public utilities.[54]

Besides freedom from labor, the 20th century bequeathed adolescents with a number of other legal rights and protections. For instance, most states set the drinking age at 21 following Prohibition,[55] the voting age was lowered from 21 to 18 in 1971,[56] and the age of consent (which stood as low as 7 in the late 19th Century) was raised, with most states setting the age at 16 or 18 by 1920.[57]

These legal mandates passed at a time when the quantity of young people rose dramatically. The post-WWII Baby Boom gave America more children than ever before. "Thanks to the rise in marriages during the war, and to general prosperity, the U.S. added 2,800,000 more consumers to its population in 1947," reported *Time* in 1948. "With an estimated population of 144 million today (v. 132 million in 1940), the U.S. has already hit a total the statisticians did not expect it to reach until the 1950s."[58]

What the Baby Boom narrative often fails to consider is the sub-

52   Hobbs, McKechnie, and Lavalette, p. 168
53   Tratter, p. 136
54   Foner and Garraty, p. 167
55   http://chnm.gmu.edu/cyh/teaching-modules/230?section=primarysources&source=24, accessed 23 May 2015
56   *The New York Times*, 26 July 1971, p. 21
57   http://chnm.gmu.edu/cyh/teaching-modules/230, accessed 26 March 2015
58   *Time*, 9 February 1948, p. 85

stantial increase in the American population happening even before the United States joined World War II. The 8 December 1941 issue of *Time* reported that "The U.S. Birth rate has hit a ten-year high in 1941, with an estimated total of 2,500,000 new babies ... which represents a gain of 140,000 babies over the 2,360,339 born last year."[59] The article cites the facts that "the large crop of babies born after the boys got back from the [first] World War have now become old enough to have babies of their own." Perhaps most presciently, it also notes that "having a family tends to keep a man out of the draft" and that "there is also a natural urge to produce offspring before being shot to pieces".[59]

However, nothing would compare to the post-WWII population explosion. "The boom," observed *Time* in 1953, "has shown no letup chiefly because World War II spurred early marriages, and high wages have made it possible to have bigger families. In addition, advances in medicine have greatly reduced the mortality rate."[60]

An article in the 1960 U.S. Census titled "Our Growing Population" shows an increase in national population from 1940 to 1950 of more than 19 million – the largest 10-year population increase in U.S. history to that point, and an average increase of not quite 2 million people per year. The same source shows an increase from 1950 to 1960 of almost 28 million – again the largest increase in history to that point, averaging not quite 3 million per year. The overall American population through those two decades increased from 132 million in 1940 to 179 million in 1960.

Some predicted that the birth rate would dwindle in the 1950s as the children born during the Great Depression (far fewer in number than the children born during the Roaring Twenties) came of age. But, as *Time* observed, elevated birth rates continued: "The fewer couples of marriageable age have been counterbalanced by the fact that high incomes and steady employment are leading couples not only to marry younger but also to have more children. ... The number of fourth children [in a single family] being born this year [1953] exceeds 1940's by 61%."[60] This population swell would have far-reaching effects on every aspect of American life and culture.

By the late 1950s and early 1960s, the first boomers had entered adolescence, becoming America's largest body of teenagers. This led to significant economic shifts as products catered to the young suddenly found larger markets. As one 1948 *Newsweek* headline proclaimed, "Ba-

---

59   *Time*, 8 December 1941, p. 37-38
60   *Time*, 14 September 1953, p. 96

bies mean business".[61] In 1953, *Time* also noted "vast increases in markets for children's and teen-agers' consumer needs."[60] And a 1958 *Variety* article with the headline "Teen Market in Vast Expansion" explained that "the 'teen' market (age 13-21) stood at 19,600,000 in 1952. Last year it rose to 21,800,000. In 1958 it's going to jump to 22,400,000 and in 1959 to 23,000,000."[62] The same article quoted economist Arno H. Johnson as saying:

> The number of persons reaching 18 years of age will start to increase substantially in 1959 – from 1960 on the increase will assume major proportions. We can soon expect increased pressure ... on the consumer market [from] the increasingly youthful aspect of the American population.[63]

As the age of the average American fell, discretionary spending rose. Defined by *Variety* as "the money available after fixed expenses have been met[, t]his spending power should reach $180,000,000,000 in 1958-59, $230,000,000,000 by 1963, and $295,000,000,000 by 1968."[63] In other words, not only were there more young people than ever before, but spare cash was also plentiful, providing American youth with substantial economic power. By the mid-1960s, teens had established societal solidarity. "We are now seeing the end of the adolescent rebellion," suggests the 13 August 1965 *New York Times Magazine*. "The teen-agers have won. Their fight was to establish the fact that they are a recognizable, distinct section of society, that they have problems peculiar to them, problems which are different from those of children and adults. ... Now they have their victory. They are accepted."[64]

Meanwhile, technology advanced as well. Television supplanted radio as the primary medium for mass communication. Television's dominance liberated radio from its prior obligation to cover the 'important' matters such as news broadcasts. Consequently, radio stations embraced entertainment in general and music specifically.

Although its origins can be traced back to the 19th Century,[65] television came of age in the late 1950s and early 1960s. In 1950, only 11% of American households (4.4 million out of 40 million) had a television; by 1960, 88% (40 million out of 44 million) had at least one.[66] These

---

61  *Newsweek*, 9 August 1948
62  *Variety*, 5 March 1958, p. 1
63  *Variety*, 5 March 1958, p. 27
64  *The New York Times Magazine*, 13 August 1965, p. 59
65  Barnouw, p. 2-7
66  Theodore H. White, p. 335

figures mean that an average of nearly 10,000 households per day received their first TV set during the course of the decade.

Moreover, Americans were using their new TV sets heavily. By 1961, the average household spent 5 hours and 22 minutes per day watching television.[67] A new line of commercial products (such as TV dinners, TV trays, and the periodical *TV Guide*) catered to this new TV culture. Appreciation for television was confirmed by a 1959 survey that asked the public which communications medium they would save if they could only keep one: 42% responded that they would save television, compared to 32% for newspapers, 19% for radio, and 4% for magazines (the remaining 3% had no opinion).[68]

By the early 1960s, television had achieved dominance in American media. From then on, the United States would be, as one book's title claims, "one nation under television".[69]

\*   \*   \*   \*   \*   \*   \*   \*   \*

Historians divide the past into eras, with each era defined by relatively similar thoughts and value systems. Common beliefs – and methods of reinforcement of those beliefs – constitute a social network in which people discover and determine their own individual and collective identities. On a large enough scale, this is termed 'culture'. When values and communicative methods change, culture, by definition, changes with them – it is the societal response to a continually changing lifestyle and environment.

Over the centuries, these lifestyles and environments have changed at progressively faster rates. Consequently, culture has also changed at progressively faster rates. The Renaissance era lasted roughly from the 14th Century to the 17th Century – plenty of time for multiple generations to live, work, and create a single overall cultural identity. If we consider a generation to last approximately 25 years, then the relatively comparable values of the Renaissance lasted long enough for about 16 generations. Similarly, the Baroque era lasted from approximately 1600-1750. While substantially shorter than the period that preceded it, that is still more than enough time for multiple generations to contribute to a single overall cultural semblance. The Classical era (about 1750 to 1825) and Romantic era (about 1825 to 1900) continue the trend. It was

---

67   J. Fred MacDonald 1985, p. 147
68   J. Fred MacDonald 1985, p. 148
69   J. Fred MacDonald 1999

only starting with the 20<sup>th</sup> Century that each new generation had different aesthetic preferences from its predecessors as each generation discovered and determined its mature values. "Times are changing so fast," noted author Evelyn Millis Duvall in 1947, "that each generation lives in a world that is only partially known to the one that precedes it or the one that follows."[70]

Independence from elders – the need to distinguish and differentiate oneself and one's convictions from established patterns of thought and procedure – is a crucial step in every person's and every generation's maturation. Some generations, however, make stronger breaks than others. The psychological wounds of a second World War in the 1940s and the serene stability of the 1950s made the 1960s ripe for revolution, and nothing was going to inhibit the Boomer generation from revealing to the world what was on its mind. "We're the young generation," sang the Monkees in 1966, summing up the decade's zeitgeist, "and we've got something to say."[71]

70    Duvall, p. 1
71    The Monkees, '(Theme from) The Monkees'

# PART 2

# Kennedy as a Symbol of Youth Culture

John Fitzgerald Kennedy, 35th president of the United States of America, was a master of public relations, and he harnessed the political marketing potential of strong public relations as well as anybody before or since. He knew exactly how to flaunt his strengths and conceal his weaknesses. In doing so, Kennedy engineered his own importance on a national scale. With the rise of television coinciding with his political ascent, the new broadcast medium offered Kennedy public relations opportunities unavailable to prior candidates, and he had the vision to take full advantage. "It was Kennedy's good fortune," observes Jonathan Gould, "to grow up in the age of film and radio and then run for the presidency at precisely the moment when television, combining the spectacle of the one medium with the intimacy of the other, was emerging as the new stage of public life in America."[72]

Television's effect on politics emphasized the importance and ubiquity of a candidate's image, how the public perceived him or her. Image has been a known and oft-manipulated quality for centuries. Kennedy, however, recognized in the dawn of television an opportunity to further hone the perception of a public figure. Previously, the creation of public image required coordinated efforts across multiple media (radio, newspapers, magazines, et cetera) each of which required helpful interpretation by reporters, editors, and distributors. Now, a literal image could be easily disseminated to millions of television watchers across the nation and the globe. People could finally see for themselves how a potential president looked, acted, and interacted with others.

Perhaps the most handsome president in American history, Kennedy consistently presented a carefully crafted telegenic image. In fact, his physical features were so symmetrical and attractive that politic-

---

72  Gould, p. 206

al cartoonist Robert Searle, who traveled with the Kennedy campaign for a while in mid-1960, found him difficult to caricature. "Kennedy's features are too balanced," quipped Searle. "All you have to work with is the hair."[73]

Kennedy revealed his understanding of the importance of television in the changing political environment in an article titled "A Force That Has Changed the Political Scene", published in the 14 November 1959 issue of *TV Guide*. "To the voter and vote-getter alike, TV offers new opportunities, new challenges and new problems," wrote Kennedy. Television has "given the American public new ideas, new attitudes, new heroes and new villains."[74] Thus, the time was right for a politician to exploit the power of this young technology and its innovative image-based presentation methods. "A new breed of candidates has sprung up on both the state and national levels," Kennedy continued. "Most of these men are comparatively young. Their youth may still be a handicap in the eyes of the older politicians – but it is definitely an asset in creating a television image people like and (most difficult of all) remember."[74]

Kennedy was also aware of television's Machiavellian potential. "It is a medium which lends itself to manipulation, exploitation and gimmicks," continued Kennedy. "It can be abused by demagogs [sic], by appeals to emotion and prejudice and ignorance. ... Political campaigns can be actually taken over by the 'public relations' experts, who tell the candidate not only how to use TV but what to say, what to stand for and what 'kind of person' to be."[74] But, Kennedy pleaded, the viewing public has the authority to shape political outcomes by weeding out such contrived deceit. "It is in your power to perceive deception, to shut off gimmickry, to reward honesty," he said. "Without your approval, no TV show is worthwhile and no politician can exist."[74]

Despite his strong words, history reveals that Kennedy's own image was largely fabricated. Though he probably believed his words and felt confident in his abilities as a leader, much of his life was in fact contrary to the veneer he conveyed. Though Kennedy's presidency is often glamorously associated with Camelot, there was, as biographer Seymour M. Hersh writes, "a dark side to Camelot, and to John Kennedy."[75]

While his appearance was of a healthy, robust, and vigorous father and family man, Kennedy suffered from an abundance of physical ailments and his political commitments often undermined his familial

---

73    *Life*, 17 October 1960, p. 76

74    *TV Guide*, 14 November 1959, p. 5-7

75    Hersh, p. ix

duties. He endured debilitating back pain for most of his life, which sometimes forced him to use crutches.[76] Naval medical records from his first spinal surgery in 1944 indicate evidence of osteoporosis which lead to three fracture vertebrae.[77] He was officially diagnosed with Addison's Disease (adrenal insufficiency) in 1947 – a fact he frequently lied about.[78] Furthermore, he had suffered from arthritis beginning as early as 1955, which so severely limited his movement that he couldn't put on his socks. Bouts of colitis and prostatitis also marred his health. From May 1955 through October 1957, he was hospitalized nine times.[79]

Photographs of Kennedy in his famous rocking chair helped establish his image as a folksy, down-home, easy-going man. However, the real reason why Kennedy sat in that rocking chair was because his doctor recommended the chair to alleviate his excruciating back pain.[80] Similarly, Kennedy's eyesight was far from perfect, but he rarely wore his glasses out of fear that spectacles made him look weak and/or old.[81]

The stress of a presidential campaign and its subsequent responsibilities only added to his ills. While in office, Kennedy suffered from insomnia, dehydration, fevers, diarrhea, urinary infections, and abscesses, among other maladies.[76] Yet during the 1,036 days of his presidency, he missed only one day of work.[82] The extensive medical care the president required prompted biographer Richard Reeves to remark: "Kennedy was more promiscuous with physicians and drugs than he was with women."[83]

Reeves' pronouncement was not made lightly. Just as Kennedy's image as a healthy, strapping young man obscured his sickly reality, so too the persona of a devoted and caring husband and father was carefully crafted to hide much of the truth from the public.

Kennedy's libido was infamously insatiable and throughout his life he regularly engaged in casual sexual encounters. While still in school, his voracious carnal appetite rewarded him with gonorrhea.[84] After graduating from Harvard University in June 1940, he briefly enrolled at the Stanford School of Business Administration in California, where his womanizing continued unabated. "Here he was – the ambas-

---

76   Dallek 2003, p. 398
77   Tennant, p. 57
78   Dallek 2003, p. 76; Hersh, p. 5
79   Dallek 2003, p. 212-13
80   Lowe 2003, p. 49
81   Lowe 2003, p. 50
82   Tennant, p. 58
83   Reeves, p. 36
84   Andersen, p. 46-47

sador's son from Harvard – rich, handsome, charming, and a best-selling author to boot," remembered a classmate. "He had his pick of any girl he wanted."[84] His apartment mate at the time was impressed as well: "He'd just look at them [women] and they'd tumble."[84] Once married, the inconvenient expectation of fidelity mattered little to him, as has been well reported, if not factually documented – especially regarding Marilyn Monroe. His rationalizing included claims of insomnia and migraines "unless I've had a lay."[85]

For the ambitious campaigner, time spent at home and with family was rare and perhaps undesirable. Kennedy's endless public responsibilities often ran counter to his domestic obligations. Sometimes Jacqueline Kennedy would accompany her husband on the road, but most of the time she stayed at home by herself. Some time later she complained of being "alone almost every weekend. It was all wrong. Politics was sort of my enemy, and we had no home life whatsoever."[86]

When Mrs. Kennedy stayed behind, Mr. Kennedy had ample opportunities for affairs. Jackie, though hurt by her unfaithful spouse, never publicly confronted her husband. As an antidote to the loneliness and relationship strain, she resumed a smoking habit left over from her school days, a practice kept hidden from public view. Secret Service agents provided a 'smoke screen' by holding lit cigarettes from which Jackie could sneak puffs. Like the president, the first lady was also adept at keeping secrets behind a charismatic veneer. "We are like two icebergs," she observed, "the public life above the water, the private life is submerged. It is a bond between us."[87]

Just as JFK did, Jackie also used television to convey a fabricated image. The first lady famously gave a televised tour of the White House, broadcast for the first time on 14 February 1962. Jackie's feminine features and extensive knowledge of American history – both on display during her tour – proved her both beautiful and intelligent. But off camera, the underside of the iceberg emerged. In between filming, she smoked incessantly and downed scotch to help her relax.[88] Had viewers seen what happened behind the scenes, Jackie's public image would have suffered. Instead, her glamorous persona made her as much of a pop culture celebrity as her husband.

Together, the Kennedys reinforced their image with their young family. At the time of their father's inauguration, Caroline Kennedy

85    Andersen, p. 39
86    Andersen, p.136
87    Andersen, p. ix
88    O'Reilly and Dugard, p. 69

(born 27 November 1957) was three years old, and John F. Kennedy, Jr. (born 25 November 1960) just three months. Patrick Bouvier Kennedy was born prematurely on 7 August 1963, and lived only two days. With that birth, 34-year-old Jackie became the first first lady to bear a child while her husband was in office since Grover Cleveland's spouse, 29-year-old Frances Folsom, bore Esther Cleveland on 9 September 1893.[89]

Although five decades of history has drawn out much of the less attractive truth behind the Kennedys' glossy image, their efforts were nonetheless extremely effective in their own time. John Kennedy's appeal to young people was a key to his political success. "The torch has been passed to a new generation,"[90] he boldly stated in his inaugural address, and he symbolized the progressive ideology on which he campaigned. The response was enormous. "His most excited following lies among the young," wrote Russell Baker in the 24 October 1960 *New York Times*. Baker went on to describe Kennedy's appeal as "adolescence's discovery of a youth symbol to sustain it".[91]

Kennedy's personal photographer, Jacques Lowe, remembered the future president often speaking at high schools during his early campaigns. "There wasn't a vote among those kids," Lowe wrote in his 1961 book *Portrait: The Emergence of John F. Kennedy*, "but when a candidate made a good impression on them, their parents were the first to hear about it."[92] While campaigning in Indiana in October 1960, *The New York Times* reported that "high school students formed a substantial part of the crowds. ... At some times they constituted half the total."[93] A survey of college campuses less than a month before the 1960 election revealed that "Republicans ... are facing an uphill fight against strong pro-Kennedy sentiment among the student bodies."[94]

Kennedy also acknowledged and respected young people to an extent that no prior presidential candidate had. "I want to express my thanks to all of you, particularly those of you who are college students and can't vote, who came down here anyway," he said on 14 October 1960 in Michigan. "I am glad you are participating actively in the political process."[95] As always, the famous Kennedy wit played into his youthful appeal. "Sometimes I wish *I* just had a summer job here,"[96] he mused to

89   Jeffers, p. 268
90   *The New York Times*, 12 January 1961, p. 8
91   *The New York Times*, 24 October 1960, section 4, p. 3
92   Lowe 1961, p. 82
93   *The New York Times*, 6 October 1960, p. 28
94   *The New York Times*, 16 October 1960, section 1, p. 73
95   Adler 1964, p. 22
96   Adler 1964, p. 58

students working in Washington D.C. during the middle months of 1962.

As his campaign grew, so did the size of his audiences and their enthusiasm. His well-established appeal to women served him well on the campaign trail. "Wherever he goes," claimed *Life* magazine, "he exerts a magic of smile and personality on women of all ages who push and shove to get close. ... All along the parade routes girls and even grown ladies were leaping and bouncing and hopping high in the air in delight at seeing Kennedy pass."[97] The same magazine would later describe "the blissful fog of feminine adoration surrounding Jack Kennedy" as "the great phenomenon of the 1960 campaign",[98] and quote Robert Searle observing that the allure was particularly strong among young women: "I remember hearing: 'All right, Margie, now you touch me and then I'll touch Jane and Jane can touch–.' Margie of course had touched Kennedy."[99]

Jacques Lowe also recalled the development of a certain degree of mania. It seemed to follow the presidential hopeful wherever he went in the months leading up to the election:

> Towards the end of the campaign the crowds became uncontrollable. ... The senator was having a curious effect on people. It was a mixture of personal magnetism and adulation. It started with women. ... Some young girls would stand and watch in silent rapture, then break into tears when Kennedy came anywhere near them. Others would howl and scream and kick their feet as soon as he smiled or asked for their help. ... After a while the men began to feel some of the candidate's appeal, too. Crowds would be silent when he began his speech, but the minute he smiled his audience began to shriek. ... At times the uproar was so great that he couldn't get his words or program across.[100]

*The New York Times* noted that "there appears to be a striking similarity between the reactions the Democratic candidate produces in the bobby-sox [young female] contingents that turn out to greet him and those evoked by Dick Clark or Frank Sinatra."[101] Sometimes the crowds would be so crazed that law enforcement struggled to contain them. "The feminine element in the crowds," continued the article, "seemed particularly imbued with a desire to touch the Senator. In many places this desire was so strong that the local police found it impossible to maintain an open lane through the crowds for the campaign caravan."[101] Some

97   *Life*, 10 October 1960, p. 28; *Life*, 31 October 1961, p. 23
98   *Life*, 11 November 1960, p. 29
99   *Life*, 31 October 1960, p. 78
100  Lowe 1961, p. 162-163, 166; Lowe 1993, p. 83
101  *The New York Times*, 2 October 1960, p. 54

of Lowe's photographs from just before the election capture the struggle.[102]

While these frenzies furthered his political celebrity and success, they also took a toll on Kennedy's already frail physical health. He frequently lost his voice due to shouting, trying to be heard over the vociferous crowds, and he began consuming medicated sugar cubes in between speeches to soothe his sore throat.[103] Kennedy's staff took to carrying extra clothing to replace that which was so often torn by fans' desperate hands.[103] He also suffered scrapes and scratches from the fingernails of women straining for a touch.[103] These troubles, and likely countless more like them which have been lost to history, are probably what Kennedy had in mind when on 14 September 1960 he said, "I personally have lived through ten Presidential campaigns, but I must say the eleventh makes me feel like I lived through twenty-five."[104] And that was nearly two months before the election!

## *"The Times They are A-Changing"*

Contrary to popular belief, Kennedy was not the youngest president. He was born 29 May 1917 and inaugurated on 20 January 1961, making him 43 years and 236 days old when he became president. But Theodore Roosevelt was born 27 October 1858 and inaugurated on 14 September 1901, making him 42 years and 322 days old – about nine months younger than JFK – when he became president. Kennedy was, however, the youngest *elected* president, as Roosevelt was vice president under William McKinley and only assumed office by succession after McKinley's assassination.

In stark contrast to the youthful Kennedy, Dwight David Eisenhower, at 70 years and 98 days, was then the country's oldest president. Thus, the age gap of 26 years and 228 days between America's 34th and 35th presidents was – and remains – by far the largest between any successive presidents in history.

With the benefit of hindsight, Kennedy and Eisenhower represented two dramatically different eras and lifestyles. Where Eisenhower's presidency put to rest the brutal Second World War, Kennedy's presidency coincided with a new, youthful era in which old societal conventions would soon be rendered obsolete – an era that would see public

---

102  Lowe 1961, p. 164-165
103  Lowe 2003, p. 188
104  Adler 1964, p. 18

availability of the birth control pill, widespread experimentation with drugs, hippies, second wave feminism, the Civil Rights Movement, and man walking on the moon. The differences between the two presidents serve as a microcosm for time periods they symbolized.

Kennedy often skinny dipped in the White House pool as a way to embrace and flaunt his masculinity, and sometimes invited colleagues and members of the media to join him.[105] He was also frequently photographed playing sports, cavorting with his children, or sailing on Cape Cod. His sunglasses gave him an air of James Dean coolness. It is difficult to imagine the septuagenarian President Eisenhower doing in any of those situations!

Kennedy's lush hair, quite long by the standards of the day, helped reinforce his youthful appearance. Here, too, JFK contrasted Ike, as one girl observed in a letter mailed to the White House:

> Dear Mr. President,
> I would like very much a lock of your hair that I can keep in my memory book.
> I never asked a President for a lock of hair before. I was going to ask President Eisenhower but then I saw he didn't have much to spare.
> Thank you in advance,
> Jennifer[106]

Lastly, the differences between Eisenhower and Kennedy can also be seen in their artistic and cultural policies. Kennedy vehemently supported the arts. "There is a connection, hard to explain logically but easy to feel, between achievement in public life and progress in the arts," wrote Senator Kennedy in a letter dated 13 September 1960. "The age of Pericles was also the age of Phidias. The age of Lorenzo de Medici was also the age of Leonardo da Vinci. The age [of] Elizabeth [was] also the age of Shakespeare. And the New Frontier for which I campaign in public life, can also be a New Frontier for American art."[107]

Upon election to the White House, Kennedy continued his support for the arts. At his inauguration, he invited fellow Pulitzer Prize winner and New Englander Robert Frost (1874-1963) to compose and read a poem for the occasion. "If more politicians knew poetry, and more poets knew politics," said Kennedy in a speech at Harvard University four and a half years earlier, "I am convinced the world would be a little

---

105  O'Reilly and Dugard, p. 33, 36
106  Adler 1965, p. 91
107  http://www.jfklibrary.org/Research/Research-Aids/Ready-Reference/JFK-Quotations.aspx, accessed 13 March 2015

better place in which to live."[107] Kennedy also invited some fifty authors, painters, and musicians – including John Steinbeck, E. B. White, W. H. Auden, and Ernest Hemingway – to attend his inauguration.[108] In addition, Kennedy regularly held cultural events at the White House: concerts, readings, recitals, dramatic performances, and recognition dinners for Spanish Cellist Pablo Casals (1876-1973) and Russian composer Igor Stravinsky (1882-1971) among others.[108]

Nobody can accuse Eisenhower of not supporting the arts (in 1955 he proposed a federal advisory council for the arts, and on 2 September 1958 signed the National Cultural Center Act[108]), but he did not place the same degree of visible emphasis on culture that Kennedy did. In fact, Kennedy's support for the arts was unprecedented among American chiefs of state. This patronage is a major reason why the John F. Kennedy Memorial Center for the Performing Arts in Washington D.C. bears his name.

But as much as Kennedy projected a progressive image, the man behind the handsome facade sometimes hesitated to actually embrace change. Most notably, at a time when the Civil Rights Movement gained momentum, the president purposely avoided exercising his political authority to help advance the cause for as long as possible. Though he did eventually endorse Civil Rights legislation, as historian Robert Dallek explains, "Kennedy had tried to avoid a showdown over civil rights, viewing it as likely to refocus too much national attention on a fiercely divisive domestic issue that could jeopardize his reelection."[109]

Despite his lukewarm attitude towards the cause, Kennedy still managed to win African-American support. When Martin Luther King, Jr. was arrested on 19 October 1960 for violating segregation laws in an Atlanta department store, Kennedy called King's pregnant wife to express concern and offer support. The gesture particularly impressed Martin Luther King, Sr., who reversed his vote as a result. "I had expected to vote against Senator Kennedy because of his religion," he said. "But now he can be my president, Catholic or whatever he is. It took courage to call my daughter-in-law at a time like this. He had a moral courage to stand up for what he knows is right."[110]

In spite of Kennedy's disinclination towards aspects of the progressive temperament of the 1960s, the public view of him remained glowingly revolutionary, and for years he was almost automatically asso-

---

108   Schlesinger, p. 730-733
109   Dallek 2013, p. 352
110   Matthews 2011, p. 310

ciated with the decade's innovations and accomplishments, if not directly credited for their success.

## Harry Truman's Boycott

Conspiracy theories about John F. Kennedy didn't start with his assassination. Nearly three and a half years before his controversial death, Kennedy was at the heart of an alleged collusion behind his selection as the Democratic presidential nominee.

On 2 July 1960, in protest to what he believed to be "a pre-arranged affair", former U.S. president Harry S. Truman announced his resignation as a Democratic national convention delegate in a national press conference.[111] In Truman's mind, Kennedy was too young and inexperienced to have legitimately earned so much delegate support; therefore, the system must be rigged. "A convention which is controlled in advance by one group and its candidate leaves the delegates no opportunity for a democratic choice and reduces the convention to a mockery," he lambasted. "I've always believed that the Democratic party should stand for an open convention and should resist any bandwagon that thwarts or stifles the free and deliberative process of this great instrument of democracy."[111] Truman continued by expressing "great regret and deep emotion" over not attending the convention – the first he missed since 1934 – "but the times are such that the future success of the party and the restoration of leadership to the nation compel me to forgo personal consideration and do whatever I can to alert the Los Angeles convention."[111]

At once understanding and patronizing, Truman also insisted that Kennedy was not personally to blame: "My disappointment at the manner in which some of the backers of Senator Joseph [sic] F. Kennedy have acted involves in no way in my mind the person or qualifications of the Senator himself."[111] Rather, the 76-year-old former president saw the 43-year-old future president as a handsome and naïve pawn being controlled by those behind the scenes, a "victim of circumstances brought on by some of his overzealous backers."[111]

At his most blunt, Truman directly addressed and challenged Kennedy's maturity, experience, and overall ability to lead the country:

> Senator, are you certain that you're quite ready for the country or the country is ready for you in the role of President in January, 1961? I've no doubt about the political heights to which you are destined to rise. But I'm deeply concerned and troubled about the situation we are up against

---

111  *The New York Times*, 3 July 1960, p. 18

in the world now and in the immediate future. That is why I hope that someone with the greatest possible maturity and experience would be available at this time. May I urge you to be patient? You will recall that I suggested to you at our meeting in Independence that all personal ambitions be put aside and that we all join forces to seek out such a man who could unite us in purpose and action. ... Let the Democratic convention nominate a man who not only can be elected but who will know what to do to pull the country out of its difficulties.[111]

Truman went on to list nine other potential Democratic presidential nominees which he apparently believed to be better qualified for the demands of the office: Missouri Senator Stuart Symington, Texas Senator Lyndon B. Johnson, Connecticut Governor Chester Bowles, New Jersey Governor Robert B. Meyner, Pennsylvania Senator Joseph Clark, Minnesota Senator Eugene J. McCarthy, Washington Senator Henry M. Jackson, Tennessee Senator Albert Gore, Minnesota Governor Orville Freeman, and Florida Governor LeRoy Collins.[111]

Truman's attack may have played directly into Kennedy's plan. Kennedy was well aware that many American citizens – and particularly older citizens – would question his young age and lack of experience. When Truman voiced those concerns through a national press conference, he represented a significant portion of the American public and provided Kennedy with the perfect opportunity for rebuttal on a national scale. On Independence Day 1960, Kennedy held his own televised press conference in response.

How something is said is just as important as what is said, and how Kennedy responded to Truman is significant. He could have adopted a reverential and penitent attitude by graciously acknowledging and accepting Truman's criticism by withdrawing from presidential consideration. But he put that idea to rest immediately: "I do not intend to step aside at anyone's request."[112] He could also have politely disagreed with Truman by calmly and respectfully supplying evidence to quash Truman's accusations. Instead, proving his courage by standing up to a well-respected former chief of state nearly twice his age, Kennedy aggressively addressed and rejected Truman's allegations: "Mr. Truman accused my supporters of using improper pressure on the delegates. Not one concrete example has ever been named. I do not want any votes that have been pressured."[112]

Kennedy proceeded to list famous Americans who contributed substantially to the nation before their 44th birthday: Thomas Jefferson

112 *The New York Times*, 5 July 1960, p. 20

was 33 years old when he helped write the Declaration of Independence, George Washington was 43 years old when he assumed command of the Continental Army, James Madison was 36 years old when he 'fathered the Constitution', Alexander Hamilton was either 32 or 34 years old (there is some dispute over what year he was born) when he served as Secretary of the Treasury, Henry Clay was 33 years old when he was elected Speaker of the House, and Christopher Columbus was 41 years old when he 'discovered' America. "This is still a young country founded by young men 184 years ago today and it is still young in heart, youthful in spirit," Kennedy proclaimed. "The average age of those who wrote the Declaration of Independence was certainly in the late thirties or early forties. The strength and health and vigor of these young men is equally needed in the White House".[112] Kennedy also pointed out that the Constitution specified the minimum age for presidential candidacy to be 35, thus Truman's notion that the age of 43 was too young was quite literally unconstitutional.

At times, Kennedy even poked fun at the former president. "Anyone who may feel that they don't have enough delegates to get nominated always says that somebody else has rigged or pre-arranged the convention," he taunted. "Based on my observations of him in 1952 and in 1956 and last Saturday, Mr. Truman regards an open convention as one which studied all the candidates, reviews their records and then takes his advice."[112] Kennedy knew that Truman had held elective office for ten years prior to assuming the office of president – four fewer years' experience than Kennedy had in comparable offices despite the fact that Truman was significantly older (61). "If we are to establish a test for the Presidency whereby fourteen years in major elective office is insufficient experience," Kennedy noted, "every President elevated to that office in the twentieth century should have been ruled out, including ... Harry Truman himself."[112]

Kennedy's confrontational response established him as recalcitrant, unwilling to take any flak from anybody – even respected elders. "It is time," he said, "for a new generation of leadership to cope with new problems and new opportunities."[112] John Hellmann, in his book *The Kennedy Obsession: The American Myth of JFK*, draws parallels between the Truman/Kennedy encounter and Western and Rebel films of the 1950s, in the process explaining how and why their exchange actually favored Kennedy by reinforcing his youthful, rebellious, and heroic image:

Kennedy transformed the political problem into a dramatic crisis evok-
ing the showdowns toward which the western movies of the day invari-
ably moved. Coming out to face Truman in the glare of the cameras, he
was translating Truman's patronizing statement into the discourse of the
western genre, walking into the open street of the town to face the vil-
lain's challenge. ... As a youth complaining of being unfairly categorized
and dismissed, Kennedy drew on his visual similarities to the sensitive
young rebels of the fifties screen – Dean, Brando, and Newman. Like the
heroes in such movies as *Rebel Without a Cause*, *The Wild One*, and *The
Left-Handed Gun*, Kennedy could win the empathy of those viewers, especially the young, who felt unfairly treated or patronized by the domin-
ant culture. ... Kennedy's heavy-lidded, detached stare and slightly iron-
ic smile also suggested the young rebel's attitude. These visual elements
reinforced Kennedy's rebellious stance in chiding an elder former president as an authoritarian.[113]

This imagery, not necessarily consciously perceived by the public, proved Kennedy's tactical brilliance and willingness to address challenges and challengers head-on. In the public perception, his aggressive
tactics helped showcase his strong leadership skills and belief in the
American political system. "I am willing," he confidently stated, "to let
our party and nation be the judge of my experience and ability."[112]

Kennedy also mentioned that, in addition to being a young man
himself, his political party was also young "from the point of view of vitality, intellectual curiosity, the willingness to recognize changing revolutionary times. I've never felt that those were qualities for which the
Republican party was particularly noted. ... They're controlled by men
who believe that the past is bright."[112]

Author and political journalist Theodore White, researching for
his 1961 book *The Making of the President 1960*, attended the Democratic national convention and noted that "a convention is an assembly of
older men, averaging in age over fifty."[114] At 43 years of age, Kennedy
would have been a proverbial spring chicken. His confrontation with
Truman just a few weeks earlier had reinforced his belief in the need for
young leaders. To that effect, Kennedy surrounded himself with like-
minded men of similar age. "Old-timers are afraid of us," said one such
young Kennedy aide. "We have to have older men like [fellow Kennedy
supporters 55-year-old John] Bailey and [51-year-old Hy] Raskin down-
stairs to deal with them, just to make them feel we're safe."[115]

White, acknowledging "the reporter's obligation ... to protect

---

113  Hellmann, p. 104
114  Theodore H. White, p. 185
115  Theodore H. White, p. 187

the privacy of those who have befriended him with information",[116] an-
onymously quoted another young Kennedy aide's description of the generation gap:

> I used to think during the war that people who stayed home in their jobs
> were getting ahead of us. There we were overseas, losing all those years.
> And there they were at home getting ahead. Now I feel sorry for the
> older men. I think we learned something during the war about how to do
> things; we learned how to work in a way the generals didn't understand.
> They'd tell us what to do, but then we had to go out and organize the
> thing – cut the red tape, get the stuff there on time, no matter how, throw
> away the rule book. We learned to work together without any fussing. ...
> We learned to work that way during the war, and I feel sorry for the
> older fellows who never learned.[115]

Though the connection was never drawn explicitly, from the point of
view of Kennedy's staff it seems Harry Truman was one of 'the older fellows who never learned.'

Despite Truman's boycott, Kennedy did receive the Democratic
nomination. In his acceptance speech on 15 July 1960, broadcast to 35
million television viewers,[117] he developed the themes discussed in his
response to Truman – namely of the challenges of progress as opposed to
the ease of the familiar. It was during this speech that Kennedy intro-
duced the slogan that would come to define his campaign:

> Today our concern must be with th[e] future. For the world is
> changing. The old era is ending. The old ways will not do. ... It is time,
> in short, for a new generation of leadership. All over the world, particu-
> larly in the newer nations, young men are coming to power – men who
> are not bound by the traditions of the past – men who are not blinded by
> the old fears and hates and rivalries – young men who can cast off the
> old slogans and the old delusions. ...
>
> I stand here tonight facing west on what was once the last fron-
> tier. From the lands that stretch 3,000 miles behind us, the pioneers gave
> up their safety, their comfort and sometimes their lives to build our new
> West. ... We stand today on the edge of a new frontier – the frontier of
> the Nineteen Sixties – the frontier of unknown opportunities and perils –
> the frontier of unfulfilled hope and unfilled threats. ...
>
> **The New Frontier** is here, whether we seek it or not. Beyond
> that frontier are uncharted areas of science and space, unsolved problems
> of peace and war, unconquered pockets of ignorance and prejudice, un-
> answered questions of poverty and surplus. It would be easier to shrink
> from that New Frontier, to look to the safe mediocrity of the past, to be
> lulled by good intentions and high rhetoric – and those who prefer that

116  Theodore H. White, p. viii
117  Theodore H. White, p. 214

course should not vote for me or the Democratic party. But I believe that the times require imagination and courage and perseverance. I'm asking each of you to be pioneers toward that New Frontier. My call is to the young in heart, regardless of age. ... The choice that our nation must make [is] a choice that lies not merely between two men or two parties, but ... between the fresh air of progress and the stale, dank atmosphere of 'normalcy' – between dedication or mediocrity. All mankind waits upon our decision. A whole world looks to see what we shall do.[118]

## The 1960 Presidential Debates

Nowhere else did Kennedy's image – artificial though it often was – aid his political success more than during the televised presidential debates. In the 21st Century, the presidential and vice presidential debates are thought of as an instrumental resource for the public to see and hear the leading candidates. In 1960, however, the concept was brand new. (Abraham Lincoln and Stephan Douglas famously debated in 1858, but that was for a spot in the senate, not for the presidency.[119]) 1960 was the first year the leading presidential candidates debated explicitly for the coming election – and they did so on television.

Kennedy's opponent in the election, then-vice president Richard Milhous Nixon, had a strong history as a debater. In his famous "Kitchen Debate" with Soviet leader Nikita Khrushchev on 24 July 1959, Nixon championed American capitalist ideals and values against those of communist governments. American reactions to televised broadcasts of the debate a day later were overwhelmingly positive. It helped establish Nixon's credibility, competence, and patriotism for the U.S. public. *Time* rewarded Nixon with a cover feature, and wrote of how he "managed in a unique way to personify a national character proud of peaceful accomplishment, sure of its way of life, confident of its power under threat."[120]

After such a spectacular episode, Nixon readily agreed to debate Kennedy a year later. But he almost immediately regretted the decision. "I'm better known than [JFK] is and I'm the front-runner," said Nixon. "By appearing with me, he'll get far greater exposure then he would on paid television time and alone. And how do I handle him? If I hit him hard, he'll have the sympathy of the audience. If I don't, then I'll look weak."[121]

As the underdog, Kennedy realized that with these debates he

---

118  *The New York Times*, 16 July 1960, p. 7

119  Carwardine p. 70 +

120  *Time*, 3 August 1959, p. 12

121  Pietrusza, p. 312

had nothing to lose and everything to gain. "Every time we get those two fellows on the screen side by side," encouraged Kennedy's aide J. Leonard Reinsch, "we're going to gain, and he's going to lose."[122] Although Kennedy had originally wanted at least five debates, and Nixon initially insisted a maximum of three, they eventually compromised and four dates were set: 26 September, 7 October, 13 October, and 21 October.[123]

As the history books now widely proclaim, Kennedy realized and embraced the political opportunities provided by television and his Republican opponent did not. "Television is not as effective as it was in 1952," said Nixon in the summer before the election. "The novelty has worn off."[124] Apparently no one let Nixon know that for the approximately 25 million households that got their first TV since 1952 (see page 14), the novelty had definitely not worn off. Journalist Richard H. Rovere pointed out in an article published in the 8 October 1960 issue of *The New Yorker* that the 1960 election was "the third Presidential campaign to be conducted mainly by means of television."[125] But even though the two prior elections had used television, the 1960 campaigns would be the first to capitalize on television's unique capacity to influence political thought on a national scale.

Understanding that significance, Kennedy ensured he was well rested and ready for battle in the first debate. "This is the way the heavyweight champion must feel when he leaves for Madison Square Garden," he remarked in the car on his way to the television studio.[126] Nixon, on the other hand, arrived after two weeks of especially stressful campaigning and was ill-prepared for the match. A few weeks earlier he had badly bruised his left knee against his limousine door while campaigning in Greensboro, North Carolina. But rather than rest, he continued campaigning, determined not to lose precious time. Eventually, however, he was hospitalized. Released on 9 September, Nixon doubled his efforts to make up for lost time. It was precisely the opposite of what he needed physically, and he continued to suffer while traveling for a further two weeks. His health gradually declined from the grueling schedule, and when he arrived in Chicago on 25 September for the following evening's first debate, he was exhausted and 10 pounds under his already trim weight.[127]

---

122 Theodore H. White, p. 339-340
123 Pietrusza p. 313; Theodore H. White, p. 339-340
124 Matthews 1996, p. 144
125 *The New Yorker*, 8 October 1960, p. 167
126 *Life*, 10 October 1960, p. 30
127 Pietrusza, p. 317-318

Upon his arrival at the studio, Nixon bruised his knee again getting out of his car. One witness observed Nixon's face turning "white and pasty" from the pain, but he once again refused to rest and continued on.[128] Inside, a moment later, he banged his head on a microphone.[129]

Nixon thus entered the first debate ailing and flustered, and his appearance showed it. Kennedy, though never far removed from serious physical ailments, appeared young, healthy, and robust, while Nixon appeared old, fatigued, and gaunt. "In a comparison of the 'image' of the two candidates," noted *The New York Times* on 28 September, "there was frequent mention of how drawn and weary the vice president had looked."[130] His mother even telephoned him after the first debate to ask if he was ill.[131]

Nixon's appearance was so haggard that accusations of subversion surfaced. "Suggestions were made that there might have been sabotage by a Democrat posing as an impartial make-up artist," reported *The New York Times*. The vice president's secretary, Herbert G. Klein, quickly dismissed the accusations,[132] but Nixon nevertheless hired a new make-up man for the second debate (insisting that it was only because the first make-up artist fell ill just before the second debate – not because of the problems from the first debate).[133]

Just before beginning the first debate, CBS producer Don Hewitt encouraged both candidates to "play to the cameras. That's where the votes are."[126] Kennedy took the advice, facing directly into the camera as if speaking to each of the millions of television viewers personally. Adding to his image problems, Nixon often spoke to his opponent instead of the viewers, in accordance with debating standards prior to TV.[134]

During that first debate, monitored by Howard K. Smith, the question of Kennedy's lack of experience surfaced yet again in the form of a question from Bob Fleming of ABC News:

> FLEMING: Senator, the Vice President in his campaign has said that you were naive and at times immature. He has raised the question of leadership. On this issue, why do you think people should vote for you rather than the Vice President?
>
> KENNEDY: Well, the Vice President and I came to the Congress togeth-

128  Theodore H. White, p. 343
129  *The New York Times*, 27 September 1960, p. 30
130  *The New York Times*, 28 September 1960, p. 26
131  Troy, p. 211
132  *The New York Times*, 1 October 1960, p. 9
133  *The New York Times*, 6 October 1960, p. 34
134  Murray, p. 92

er [in] 1946; we both served in the Labor Committee. I've been there now for fourteen years, the same period of time that he has, so our experience in government is comparable. ...

SMITH: Mr. Nixon, would you like to comment on that statement?

NIXON: I have no comment.[135]


Unfortunately for his election hopes, Nixon had apparently forgotten his own campaign slogan, "Experience Counts".[136] Nixon's declining comment and his anemic television presence effectively turned his slogan from a laurel into a liability. Arthur Brock summarized the public perception in *The New York Times* shortly thereafter:

> Though Nixon is only four years Kennedy's senior (47 in January, 1960), he makes the visual impression of being more than that. And while his emphasis on 'experience' is to impress on the electorate a training in high-level administration Kennedy has not had, the very word suggests advanced years in public mind. Kennedy's counter has been to attract the people with the combination he claims of both youth and experience.[137]

Despite the candidates' similar ages and experience, Kennedy turned the tables by pointing out that his and Nixon's political ideals differed in age. "The Republican nominee, of course, is a young man," he admitted in his Democratic nomination acceptance speech. "But his approach is as old as McKinley. His party is the party of the past – the party of memory. His speeches are generalities from Poor Richard's Almanac. Their platform, made up of old left-over Democratic planks, has the courage of our old convictions."[138] Where Nixon reeked of The Old, Kennedy sparkled with The New.

Kennedy responded to Nixon's, Truman's, and others' accusations of lack of experience with his customary humor. "Experience," mocked JFK, "is what he [Nixon] will have left after this campaign is over."[139] He frequently told anecdotes throughout his campaign to illustrate his point: "I know a banker who served thirty years as president of a bank," he mused in an October 1960 speech in Jacksonville, Florida. "He had more experience, until his bank went broke, than any other banker in Massachusetts. But if I ever go in the banking business, I do not plan

---

135 http://www.debates.org/index.php?page=september-26-1960-debate-transcript, accessed 22 March 2015
136 Matthews 1996, p. 153
137 *The New York Times*, 2 October 1960, section 4, p. 11
138 *The New York Times*, 16 July 1960, p. 7
139 Adler 1964, p. 25

to hire him, and he knows the operation from top to bottom."[140]

The senator said something similar in a speech from the twentieth day of that same month in Minneapolis, Minnesota: "The outstanding news story of this week was not the events of the United Nations or even the Presidential campaign. It was a story coming out of my own city of Boston that Ted Williams of the Boston Red Sox had retired from baseball. It seems that at forty-two he was too old. It shows that perhaps experience isn't enough."[141]

The Kennedy/Nixon debates have been analyzed extensively since their broadcast and awarded legendary status, but the immediate responses were inconclusive. The day after the first debate, *The New York Times* reported that "most of the audience apparently made one of two basic decisions: their vote preferences remained unchanged, or they were still very much undecided."[142] The next day, the same newspaper ran the headline, "TV Debate Switched Few Votes, Nation-Wide Survey Shows".[143] A nearly identical headline followed the next debate: "Second Nation-Wide Study Shows Few Voters Are Changing Sides".[144] And a similar one followed the third: "Survey of TV Viewers Calls the Debate a Draw; Few Voters Said to Find Cause to Shift Votes".[145] Regarding the fourth, "a survey in more than a score of cities throughout the country indicated that the public considered the fourth debate – and, indeed, their whole series of four debates – substantially a draw. ... Remarkably few voters said that they had changed their allegiance because of the debates."[146]

These findings are in stark contrast to those reported by Theodore White in his 1961 book *The Making of the President 1960*. White referenced a poll conducted after the fourth debate that found that 57% indicated that the debates had influenced their vote. An additional 6% reported that their vote was based solely on the debates. Of that 6%, 26% had voted for Nixon while 72% had voted for Kennedy.[147]

While the true scope and extent of how the debates influenced voters may never be conclusively determined, Kennedy himself believed the debates – and specifically that they were televised – to have been instrumental in his success. "It was the TV more than anything else that

---

140 Adler 1964, p. 12

141 Adler 1964, p. 13

142 *The New York Times*, 27 September 1960, p. 1

143 *The New York Times*, 28 September 1960, p. 26

144 *The New York Times*, 9 October 1960, section 1, p. 59

145 *The New York Times*, 15 October 1960, p. 12

146 *The New York Times*, 23 October 1960, p. 70

147 Theodore H. White, p. 353

turned the tide [of the election]," said JFK on 12 November 1960, four days after his victory.[147]

Kennedy continued to exploit television once in the White House. Having grown up in the era of FDR's famous Fireside Chat radio broadcasts, he understood the necessity of rendering the presidency and the issues of the day accessible to the public. Kennedy accomplished this through television. He was the first president to regularly deliver live broadcasts, giving 19 speeches and 14 news conferences while in office.[148]

## The Peace Corps

Like his reliance on television, Kennedy's belief in the youth of the nation also continued into his White House residency. This can be seen most clearly in his initiation of the Peace Corps. Though Kennedy did not invent the idea (there were similar proposals throughout the 1950s), he was the public figurehead of the project. His appeal to young people and the concept of a youth-oriented Peace Corps were a natural fit.

Kennedy first voiced the concept in a 14 October 1960 speech on the campus of the University of Michigan at Ann Arbor. He had just debated Nixon for the third time the previous evening. Curiously, unlike the other debates, the third saw Kennedy in New York while Nixon was in California – literally a cross-country debate. Because New York lies three time zones ahead of California, the debate occurred three hours later in the day for Kennedy than it did for Nixon, which meant late-night travel to the Democrat's next campaign stop. He arrived at the University of Michigan in the wee hours of the morning. Nevertheless, some 10,000 students were waiting for a chance to see and hear the candidate. So popular was Kennedy that the university even suspended its 11:00 p.m. curfew for female students.[149] Though exhausted, Kennedy knew the value of the opportunity and gave an impromptu three-minute speech to the college crowd:

> How many of you who are going to be doctors, are willing to spend your days in Ghana? Technicians or engineers, how many of you are willing to work in the Foreign Service and spend your lives traveling around the world? On your willingness to do that, not merely to serve one year or two years in the service, but on your willingness to contribute part of your life to this country, I think will depend the answer [of] whether a free society can compete. I think it can! And I think Americ-

148   J. Fred MacDonald 1985, p. 156-157
149   Meisler, p. 4

ans are willing to contribute. But the effort must be far greater than we have ever made in the past.

Therefore, I am delighted to come to Michigan, to this university, because unless we have those resources in this school, unless you comprehend the nature of what is being asked of you, this country can't possibly move through the next 10 years in a period of relative strength.

So I come here tonight to go to bed! But I also come here tonight to ask you to join in the effort. ...

This University is not maintained by its alumni, or by the state, merely to help its graduates have an economic advantage in the life struggle. There is certainly a greater purpose, and I'm sure you recognize it. Therefore, I do not apologize for asking for your support in this campaign. I come here tonight asking your support for this country over the next decade.[150]

A commemorative plaque at the location now reads:

Here at 2:00 a.m. on October 14, 1960, John Fitzgerald Kennedy first defined the Peace Corps.[151]

But Kennedy never actually used the term 'Peace Corps' in this speech. Furthermore, *The New York Times*, which covered his campaign extensively, wrote that "Mr. Kennedy, to be sure, said nothing that was new"[152] during his Michigan visit. While that appears inaccurate (it was, in fact, the first time he had mentioned anything like the Peace Corps) it is clear from contemporary sources that little was thought of the idea at the time. Regardless, it was the first instance of the presidential hopeful ever publicly discussing the concept that would eventually evolve into the Peace Corps. Apparently it made quite an impression on those in attendance. Following the speech, volunteer pledges inundated the Democratic headquarters in Washington D.C.[153] The show of support was so strong that Kennedy decided to pursue the concept further.

On 2 November 1960, six days before the election, Kennedy delivered a speech at the Cow Palace in San Francisco (significantly, in Nixon's home state of California) in which he *did* use the term 'Peace Corps':

We can push a button to start the next war – but there is no push-button magic to bring a just and lasting peace. ... The hard, tough work of laying the groundwork for peace must be done by thousands of hands. ...

---

150  http://www.peacecorps.gov/about/history/speech/, accessed 21 March 2015
151  Meisler, p. 5
152  *The New York Times*, 15 October 1960, p. 1
153  Meisler, p. 7

There is not enough money in all America to relieve the misery of the under-developed world in a giant and endless soup kitchen. But there is enough know-how and enough knowledgeable people to help those nations help themselves. I therefore propose that our inadequate efforts in this area be supplemented by a 'peace corps' of talented young men willing and able to service their country in this fashion for three years.[154]

In order to establish a need for the Peace Corps, Kennedy spoke of how Communist missionaries permeated the developing world. "Diplomats skilled in the languages and customs of the nation to whom they are accredited – teachers, doctors, technicians and experts desperately needed in a dozen fields by under-developed nations – are pouring forth from Moscow to advance the cause of world communism," he said. "They can only be countered by Americans equally skilled and equally dedicated. ... I am convinced that our young men and women, dedicated to freedom, are fully capable of overcoming the efforts of Mr. Khruschev's missionaries who are dedicated to undermining that freedom."[154]

Those sent by the U.S. to counter the communist missionaries so far had been ineffective, Kennedy insisted, because of cultural barriers. "A man who is ignorant of foreign languages," he quoted Goethe, "is ignorant of his own. ... We cannot understand what is in the minds of other peoples or help them understand ours if we cannot understand their language."[154] Therefore, Peace Corps members would be educated in the customs, languages, and cultures of the nations where they would be sent to help.

Of course, such a program, should it compensate its members, would be prohibitively expensive. So Kennedy requested volunteers. "They will receive no salary. Instead they will be given an allowance which will only be sufficient to meet their basic needs and maintain health," he explained. "At the conclusion of their tours, members of the Peace Corps will receive a small sum in the form of severance pay based on length of service abroad, to assist them during their first weeks back in the United States."[155]

Kennedy made no effort to sugarcoat the challenges awaiting any volunteers. "Peace Corps members will often serve under conditions of physical hardship, living under primitive conditions among the people of developing nations," he said. "It is essential that Peace Corps men and women live simply and unostentatiously among the people they have

---

154 *The New York Times*, 3 November 1960, p. 32
155 *The New York Times*, 2 March 1961, p. 13

come to assist."[155]

With such gritty descriptions, one might wonder why anybody would commit to such a program. Many young men and women seemed to volunteer just because Kennedy had asked them to. Although Dwight Eisenhower had been a revered military commander and popular president, he was neither known for such idealism, nor the sheer charisma to inspire volunteers in America and around the world. In contrast, Kennedy's personality alone seemed to drive the Peace Corps to enormous success. For some time, Peace Corps volunteers in Latin American countries were called "los hijos de Kennedy [Kennedy's children]".[156]

Kennedy's target audience for this unglamorous volunteer commitment was primarily the youth of America. "This nation is full of young people eager to serve the cause of peace in the most useful way," Kennedy said.[154] This call resonated strongly with the generation that idolized him. "There is little doubt that the number of those who wish to serve will be far greater than our capacity to absorb them,"[155] continued Kennedy. He cited "strong support from universities, voluntary agencies, student groups, labor unions and business and professional organizations" and "an enthusiastic response by student groups, professional organizations and private citizens everywhere – a convincing demonstration that we have in this country an immense reservoir of dedicated men and women willing to devote their energies and time and toil to the cause of world peace and human progress."[155]

As with his other speeches, Kennedy ended his Peace Corps proposal address with a call to action, enticing and encouraging the energetic youth of America to change the world:

> These proposals [of the Peace Corps] offer no quick and easy solution to the problems of peace. But they are essential tools. 'Give me a fulcrum,' Archimedes is reported to have said, 'and a place to stand – and I will move the world.' The tools I have suggested can be our fulcrum – it is here we take our stand – let us move the world down the road to peace. … The generation for which I speak has seen enough of war-mongers – let our great role in history be that of peacemakers.[154]

The political brilliance of the Peace Corps was its blending of two critical themes of Kennedy's presidency: (1) combating the threat of a global spread of communism and (2) harnessing the vigor of youth through his personal appeal to young people.

---

156  Meisler, p. 11

## Kennedy's Death and America's Mourning

Because of Kennedy's stature as a prominent symbol of Youth Culture, his death strongly affected America's young people. In early April 1964, not yet five months after the 22 November 1963 assassination, a conference of academics and psychologists was held at Albert Einstein College of Medicine in New York City with the purpose of evaluating children's reactions to the president's death. A compendium of their findings, published a year later under the title *Children and the Death of the President*, articulates why Kennedy appealed so much to American youth:

> A major change that occurs in the course of adolescence is the gradual and difficult withdrawal of feelings from the parents and the quest for new love objects and ideal models. It is at this time that a whole range of glamorous figures – heroes and idols from beyond their personal world in time and place – engage the emotions of young people. In this phase one would expect the transfer of some strong feelings to the President. Thus we would anticipate a sense of loss and grief for his death more in adolescents. ... [He] had a particularly strong appeal for this age group. He seemed close to them, someone who could understand them; for the younger adolescents, an ideal parent figure, for the older ones, the model of what they should strive to become. ...
>
> For young adolescents we would predict that it [Kennedy's assassination] will be remembered by many as their first experience of grief. It was for them an initiation into the experience of painful loss which none escapes in life. ... For older adolescents it meant the sudden tragic end of a career with which they were much identified. There was a young President to whom they felt unusually close. They wanted him to succeed; they felt empathetic hurt in his fall.[157]

After Kennedy's death, idealization of him was widespread, particularly among the young. "Our studies show that children and adolescents felt more positively toward [Kennedy after his death] than they had before," continued the authors of *Children and the Death of the President.* "Those who had some negative feelings tended to change over. Those who were already attached to him experienced a strengthening of this attachment."[158]

Embellishing the late president was not limited to young people. Some voting adults apparently shifted allegiance, as well. A survey conducted shortly after his death found that 65% of those polled claimed

---

157 Wolfenstein, p. xxiii, 197, 207
158 Wolfenstein, p. 205

that they had voted for Kennedy.[159] But the 1960 election was one of the closest in history, with the actual statistic of those casting ballots for the democrat being only 49.7%.[160]

This public glorification of Kennedy was enhanced by those who were closest to him. As Robert Dallek describes, wife Jackie, brother Robert, assistant Arthur Schlesinger, and adviser/speechwriter Ted Sorensen "launched a campaign to promote a romanticized picture of a heroic leader selflessly serving the nation's best interests."[161]

"Jackie Kennedy appeared less interested in theories of the assassination," comments Larry J. Sabato in *The Kennedy Half-Century*, "than in strategies to make sure that John F. Kennedy would be forever remembered as a great president."[162] Jackie put her own considerable PR skills to work by basing her husband's funeral on Abraham Lincoln's. As the 6 December 1963 issue of *Life* reports:

> Mrs. Kennedy asked someone to telephone a friend and send him to an upstairs library in the White House to get a specific book on Lincoln which contained photographs and drawings of ceremonies surrounding the lying-in-state and the funeral. ... She wanted everything now to correspond as nearly as possible to what had been done for Lincoln. She even specified that the catafalque upon which the coffin would lie in the East Room should duplicate Lincoln's.[163]

The same issue of *Life* also included an article authored by Theodore White, based on an interview with the former first lady. In it, she rhapsodizes on the Broadway musical Camelot, based on the King Arthur legends, a symbol henceforth associated with her husband's presidency:

> At night, before we'd go to sleep, Jack liked to play some records; and the song he loved most came at the very end of this record. The lines he loved to hear were: "Don't let it be forgot, that once there was a spot, for one brief shining moment that was known as Camelot." ... There'll be great Presidents again ... but there'll never be another Camelot.[164]

Americans' perceived intimacy with the Kennedy family is seen in the overwhelming quantity of sympathy letters mailed to Jackie following the assassination. By the end of 1963, she had received some

159  Manchester, p. 505
160  Theodore H. White, p. 461
161  Dallek 2013, p. 422
162  Sabato, p. 30
163  *Life*, 6 December 1963, p. 48
164  *Life*, 6 December 1963, p. 158

800,000 letters; by the end of 1965, over 1,500,000.[165]

One such letter was addressed to "First Lady in our hearts."[166] Another acknowledged that "we lost our leader, our hope for a better world within our own lifetime. They did the same thing to Christ, to Lincoln – and now Kennedy – may God help us in this hour of great darkness – our faith must be strong as Kennedy's was."[167] One woman wrote how "As no other First Family has done, you all have come into our homes and touched our personal lives, across the breadth of America. Your voices, your faces, your thoughts, your daily activities ... were personalized for us."[168] One schoolboy put the same sentiment into rather simpler words: "He was my friend even though he didn[']t know me."[169]

\* \* \* \* \* \* \* \*

There are two basic strategies for coping with a death. The first is to break all ties with the deceased. "'Letting go' refers to the act of turning to new encounters, trusting in the future," writes Catherine Sanders in her book *Grief: The Mourning After*. "This establishes expectations that move toward the rebuilding of a life."[170] It doesn't mean forgetting about the lost person (which would negate the meaning of the deceased's life) but rather learning to live without him or her, and continuing life without prolonged attachment. In that sense, any lingering relationship with the memory of the deceased is unhealthy because it interferes with the making of new connections.

The alternative method is to actively maintain connection with the deceased, as if the lost person's spirit remains after his/her physical body is gone. "Remaining connected seemed to facilitate both adults' and children's ability to cope with the loss and the accompanying changes in their lives," observed counselors Phyllis R. Silverman and Dennis Klass in their book *Continuing Bonds: New Understandings of Grief*.[171] In that sense, any lingering relationship with the memory of the deceased is healthy because it "provide[s] solace, comfort and support, and ease[s] the transition from the past to the future."[171]

These basic approaches to grief recovery – or some combination

---

165  Fitzpatrick, inside front jacket cover
166  Fitzpatrick, p. 12
167  Fitzpatrick, p. 53
168  Fitzpatrick, p. xi-xii
169  Fitzpatrick, p. 22
170  Sanders, p. 94
171  Klass, Silverman, and Nickman, p. xviii

thereof – are typically the two that mourners adopt. With Kennedy's death, those able to move forward without prolonged attachment did so. And yet for some – millions of Americans – a degree of continued attachment was needed. Helen Fitzgerald, in her book *The Grieving Teen: A Guide for Teenagers and Their Friends,* helps explain why:

> It is easy to dismiss as trivial the sadness that you feel when someone you greatly admire has died. What you must realize, though, is that this grief comes from the loss of something in yourself: the person who died was part of you, part of what you see in yourself. Others may not see that, but you do. It's all part of the continuing process of shaping your own personality, deciding how you want to look and act, and determining what you want to do in life – your creation of the person others will come to know as you.[172]

John F. Kennedy was more than just remembered by many of those who survived him, he was internalized – he became a part of American identity both on personal and political levels. When he died, a part of America died, too. Although the entire nation was wounded by his loss, young people felt this loss particularly strongly as Youth Culture suddenly lost a major figurehead. But, as Sonny & Cher would sing in 1967, "History has turned the page. ... The beat goes on."[173]

---

172  Fitzgerald, p. 138-139
173  Sonny and Cher, 'The Beat Goes On'

# PART 3

# The Beatles as Symbols of Youth Culture

A typical Beatles' concert in the U.S. included girls screaming, fainting, and even wetting themselves. That was all part of the hysterics that defined Beatlemania. But the four Liverpuddlians were the latest – not the first – to chart with their version of concert chaos. For many years, performers have elicited worship by rapturous fans. Eight years before the Fab Four reached American soil in 1964, a truck driver from Tupelo, Mississippi named Elvis Aaron Presley had excited his audience to the point of much the same madness.

### Presley-mania

After a Presley concert in La Crosse, Wisconsin on 14 May 1956, *The La Crosse Tribune* featured a front-page review of the performance under the headline "Teen-age Bedlam Greets Stomping Elvis Presley". The article described "a full house yell[ing] like wild banshees. ... When the 'king' walked onto the stage, bedlam broke loose. At the first tap of the Presley leg, the auditorium almost exploded."[174] A week later, following a performance in Sioux City, Iowa on 23 May, *The Sioux City Journal* reported that "An hysterical crowd of 5,000 gave Elvis Presley a scream-ing reception. ... The singing can barely be heard above the crowd noise for every paroxysm brings a fresh outbreak of shrieks from the audience. ... They were almost all teenagers, with girls in the overwhelming ma-jority."[175] *Time* reported that a man who had interviewed Presley was later mobbed by fans who screamed, "Touch him! Maybe he's touched Elvis!"[176] When Bea Ramirez, a reporter for the *Waco News-Tribune*, bluntly asked Elvis about the fan insanity he inspired, Presley sincerely

---

174  *La Crosse Tribune*, 15 May 1956, p. 1
175  *The Sioux City Journal*, 24 May 1956
176  *Time*, 14 May 1956, p. 53

professed ignorance:

> RAMIREZ: Elvis, have you any idea just what it was that started the girls going crazy over you?
>
> PRESLEY: No, I don't. I guess it's just something God gave me.[177]

But even before Elvis, there was a Big Band entertainer whose suave singing brought his young fans to frenzy.

### Sinatra-mania

A decade before Elvis, Francis Albert Sinatra caused rousing audience reactions. "The sound that greeted me," Sinatra recalled of an early escapade of Sinatra-mania, "was absolutely deafening, a tremendous roar. Five thousand kids, stamping, yelling, screaming, applauding. They let out a yell and I thought the roof would come off. I was scared stiff."[178] And Sinatra wasn't just 'blowing his own horn'. An article in *The New York Times* observed that "the 7,000 persons in the audience ... were mostly young. ... Their gleeful whoops, loud laughter and handclaps frequently almost drowned out the sad, sweet music of the singer."[179] When Sinatra performed in Manhattan in October 1944, fans swarmed the streets, blocking traffic and disrupting the entire city. "We don't want this thing to go on," said George H. Chatfield, a member of the Manhattan Board of Education, "We can't tolerate young people making a public display of losing control of their emotions."[180] One can't help wondering if Chatfield was still in New York two decades later! Sinatra's fame was so great that he was forced to keep the shades down in his hotel rooms "so he would not absent-mindedly show his face and throw the girls in the street below into an impromptu swoon."[180] He also was forced to eat his meals in his hotel room because "the crowds had become so big [that] he could no longer go out."[180]

Although both Frank Sinatra and Elvis Presley gave rise to fanaticism similar to that inspired by the Beatles, the sociological phenomenon of musicians prompting mass hysteria can be traced back even further.

---

177 Guralnick, p. 269
178 Sinatra, p. 52
179 *The New York Times*, 4 August 1943, p. 14
180 *The New York Times*, 13 October 1944, p. 21

## *Lisztomania*

Receding in history more than a century before The King of Rock 'n' Roll or Ol' Blue Eyes shows all this hoopla was familiar even to composers of what is now considered 'classical' music. Perhaps the earliest such example was the Hungarian pianist Franz Liszt (1811-1886), whose virtuosic recitals prompted a similar degree of delirium, as biographer Alan Walker describes:

> Liszt arrived in Berlin just before Christmas 1841. ... His first recital took place in the Berlin Singakademie on December 27. ... The clamour which erupted shook the Singakademie to its foundations and set the tone for the rest of his stay. It was at Berlin that 'Lisztomania' swept in. ...
> The symptoms ... bear every resemblance to an infectious disease, and merely to call them mass hysteria hardly does justice to what actually took place. His portrait was worn on brooches and cameos. Swooning lady admirers attempted to take cuttings of his hair, and they surged forward whenever he broke a piano string in order to make it into a bracelet. Some of these insane female 'fans' even carried glass phials about their persons into which they poured his coffee dregs. Others collected his cigar butts, which they hid in their cleavages.
> The overtones were clearly sexual. Psychologists may have a wonderful time explaining such phenomena, but they cannot change the facts: Liszt had taken Berlin by storm.[181]

Allan Kozinn lent credence to the notion of fans collecting Liszt's cigar butts in the preface of his book, *The Beatles*:

> I was nine years old when 'I Want to Hold Your Hand' and 'She Loves You' began to be heard ceaselessly on American radio ... I was devoting my own musical energies to classical music, and was studying the piano with a woman whose father had been a pupil of Liszt - and who kept a collection of Liszt's cigar butts, framed in her studio.[182]

And yet, Beatlemania surpassed all of these historical precedents, prompting one *Washington Post* writer to describe Beatlemania as "a demonstration that Elvis Presley must have contemplated with gloomy envy."[183] What elevated the mania of Beatlemania to unprecedented levels was (1) media coverage, and (2) technology. Had audio and visual recordings existed in the 1840s, perhaps Lisztomania would have been as big as Beatlemania was 12 decades later. But instead of technological

---

181  Walker, p. 371-372
182  Kozinn, p. 6
183  *The Washington Post*, 11 February 1964, p. A14

propagation, Lisztomania could only spread by word of mouth and news-papers. The careers of Elvis Presley and Frank Sinatra were both supple-mented by audio recordings, but television was still in its infancy and re-latively few Americans owned television sets compared to when Beatle-mania exploded. The band came along at precisely the right time to cap-italize on these advances in technology.

### *"The Times They are A-Changing"*

The Beatles also arrived at a time when the values of the recent past were starting to break down. After a decade of Cold War gridlock and the dawning recognition of injustice within their own countries, young Americans and Brits began to challenge ingrained traditions and values at home. The Beatles saw this as an opportunity. "Changing a life-style and the appearance of youth didn't just happen," acknowledged John Lennon. "We set out to do it."[184]

"The Beatles represent authentic British youth," claimed one news report from late 1963, "or British youth as it would like to be: self-confident, natural, direct, decent, vital, throbbing."[185] And Beatlemaniacs responded: "We screamed," acknowledged one English fan, "because it was a kick against anything old-fashioned."[186] "They're different," claimed another. "They're just so different."[187] And in her 1973 memoir *Looking Back: A Chronicle of Growing Up Old in the Sixties*, Joyce Maynard described her reaction to hearing 'I Want to Hold Your Hand' for the first time: "it seemed as if a new color had been invented. ... They [the Beatles] made kids part of history. ... Through the Beatles' existence we [young people] held some sort of control, we could act. Their appear-ance gave us our first sense of youth as a power."[188]

The first chance Americans had to see the Beatles was on 18 November 1963, when NBC broadcast a four-minute story on its evening news program. NBC's website reports that all film footage of that broad-cast has been lost, but the audio has survived. "The sound they make is called 'The Mersey Sound' because Liverpool is on the Mersey River," ex-plained the clip's voiceover. An excerpt from a live show the Beatles played in Bournemouth yields near-deafening screams that drown out much of the music. "The *London Times* has carried the sobering report

184  Stark, p. 9
185  Spizer, p. 61
186  Stark, p. 10
187  *The New York Times*, 8 February 1964, p. 25
188  Maynard, p. 34

that the Beatles may bring their 'Mersey Sound' to the United States," the voiceover continued snidely, "to which it may be rejoined: 'Show us no Mersey'."[189]

CBS also put together a brief and not entirely respectful news clip which aired first on 22 November 1963 – just hours before Kennedy's death – as part of the *CBS Morning News with Mike Wallace* and then again on 10 December on the *CBS Evening News with Walter Cronkite*.[190] The program asserts that the Mersey Sound "is no different from Rock 'n' Roll, except maybe louder", to which the Beatles agreed:

> QUESTION: What is the Mersey Sound? How does it differ from other Rock 'n' Roll and pop?
>
> GEORGE: It doesn't really. It's just happened that all of a sudden hundreds of rock groups all from Liverpool made records. And it was a bit more like the original Rock 'n' Roll than the stuff they've had over the last few months. So people decided suddenly, you know, with all these Liverpool groups, so they called it the "Liverpool Sound" and the "Mersey Beat" and everything else. Yeah, but it's just...
>
> PAUL: It's just a way of classifying it, but I don't think the music is very different.[185]

While Paul and George's comments are no doubt sincere, with the benefit of hindsight they're not entirely accurate. While the genre of 1960s English rock was heavily influenced by the genre of 1950s American Rock 'n' Roll, there are pronounced distinctions.

### 1950s American Rock 'n' Roll vs. 1960s British Rock

The primary innovation of Rock 'n' Roll was social rather than musical. It combined white American culture (Country & Western) with black American culture (Rhythm & Blues), and in doing so represented a merger between races – both contributed to the birthing of this new genre at a time when the nation was strongly segregated.

However, precisely because of the racial chasm, this fusing of black and white American cultures inevitably benefited white recording artists more it did than black ones. When Dewey Phillips interviewed 19-year-old Elvis Presley on radio on 8 July 1954, Phillips made a point of asking where Presley went to high school. This proved to their listen-

---

189  http://www.nbcnews.com/nightly-news/what-you-dont-know-about-beatles-u-s-de-but-n24171, accessed 8 April 2015

190  Spizer p. 60

ing audience that Elvis was white despite his black-sounding records.[191] And when Little Richard released 'Tutti Frutti' in 1956, it was a major hit, but, largely because of his skin color, white audiences shunned his music. Both Elvis Presley and Pat Boone subsequently covered 'Tutti Frutti', and it was their recordings that were deemed acceptable. Nearly three decades later, Little Richard described the problem:

> They didn't want me to be in the white guys' way. I felt I was pushed into a rhythm and blues corner to keep out of rockers' way, because that's where the money is. When 'Tutti Frutti' came out, Elvis was immediately put on me, dancing and singing my songs on television. They needed a rock star to block me out of white homes because I was a hero to white kids. The white kids would have Pat Boone upon the dresser and me in the drawer 'cause they liked *my* version better, but the families didn't want me because of the *image* that I was projecting.[192]

Whether considered collaboration or appropriation, Rock 'n' Roll helped break down racial barriers and anticipated the Civil Rights Movement of the subsequent decade. Consequently, the music tended to be rather primitive because social change between races – not musical sophistication – was an underlying factor.

On the other hand, because British Rock stemmed from England (where racial tensions were faint compared to those in America), breaking down racial barriers was less of a factor. Rock artists generally put more energy and effort into musical development and progress. Consequently, Rock tended to be more musically sophisticated than Rock 'n' Roll.

There were also major differences in the attitudes behind the two genres. American Rock 'n' Roll didn't care if you liked it or not – in fact, it thrived on lack of respect. British Rock, by contrast, wanted to be liked and respected. Rock took Rock 'n' Roll and elevated it into an art form by supplementing the standard Rock 'n' Roll guitar band instrumentation with classical and exotic instruments (e.g. the string quartet on 'Yesterday', the sitar on 'Norwegian Wood') and by expanding the scope and possibilities of popular music (e.g. the concept album *Sgt. Pepper's Lonely Hearts Club Band*). This gave Rock a mainstream understanding and appeal that the disreputable Rock 'n' Roll neither had nor desired.

In the late 1950s, a variety of events and circumstances lead to the downfall of Rock 'n' Roll. Several major artists had stopped recording

---

191  Guralnick, p. 101
192  *The Washington Post*, 12 November 1984, p. C13

by the end of the decade: In 1957, Little Richard denounced his immoral Rock 'n' Roll lifestyle to pursue a life in ministry.[193] In 1958, Elvis Presley was drafted into the military.[194] That same year, 22-year-old Jerry Lee Lewis married his 13-year-old cousin, causing a public scandal that effectively banished him from the business.[195] 1959 saw 'The Day the Music Died', in which superstar recording artists Buddy Holly, Ritchie Vallens, and The Big Bopper all died in a plane crash,[196] along with the arrest and imprisonment of Chuck Berry for violating the Mann Act,[197] which "outlawed the interstate transportation of women for immoral purposes."[198] Then, in 1960, Rockabilly superstars Eddie Cochran and Gene Vincent suffered a car crash that killed Cochran and severely injured Vincent, crippling both his body and career.[199]

The demise of these on-stage Rock 'n' Rollers coincided with the off-stage Payola scandal, in which Rock 'n' Roll radio DJs were accused of accepting bribes in return for promotional broadcasts of certain songs.[200] While payola was by no means a new phenomenon, the late 1950s saw a widespread effort to curb the practice and disgrace certain media tastemakers. Many then and now saw the scandal as a mere excuse to rein in the power of Rock 'n' Roll DJs to distribute their scandalous and dangerous music to American youth. To some degree, it worked: As a result of the payola scandals, radio companies leashed their DJs and standardized promotional methods to favor less controversial musical styles. By the turn of the decade, the losses of both marketing power and the genre's best artists effectively concluded the pinnacle of Rock 'n' Roll

But the transfer from Rock 'n' Roll to Rock was not immediate. There was a period of 'down time' in between during which the *Billboard* charts were dominated by insipid #1 hits such as The Singing Nun's 'Dominique'[201] and Bobby Vinton's 'There! I've Said It Again'.[202] When the Beatles took America by storm in early 1964, it brought a degree of vitality back to the nation's pop scene.

While hardly the first to capitalize on the energy of youthful audiences and fans, the Beatles were one of the first to make Rock 'n'

---

193  Charles White, p. 91-92
194  Evans, p. 599
195  Fryd, p. 78
196  Laing, p. 161
197  Collis, p. 101
198  Wayne, p. 149
199  Covach, p. 90
200  Covach, p. 94-95
201  *Billboard*, 14 December 1963, p. 24
202  *Billboard*, 18 January 1964, p. 18

Roll acceptable – or at least more acceptable than it had been. Many early American Rock 'n' Roll pioneers felt threatening and dangerous to general public audiences. Elvis Presley's emphatic sneer and suggestive his hip thrusts were scandalous, hence the nickname "Elvis the Pelvis". But where Presley moped over heartbreak and hound dogs, the Beatles celebrated adolescent puppy love and holding your hand. Their perceived innocence contributed to their appeal.

Audiences from their 1960-62 Hamburg residencies certainly would not have thought of the Beatles as innocent. Playing night clubs in the red light district of one of the most decadent cities in Europe, the band had to find ways to engage their rowdy, inebriated audiences. So they all bought black leather outfits, which provided the air of a motorcycle gang, and, fueled by copious stimulants and beer galore, they tried to be as obnoxious and offensive as possible on stage. "John used to dance around like a gorilla," George Harrison recalled in *The Beatles Anthology*, "and we'd all knock our heads together and things like that."[203] Lennon would often shout "*Sieg Heil!*" and call his audience "fucking Nazis!"[204] Had the band acted like that during their Ed Sullivan shows, Beatles history would be very different.

The Beatles established their gritty image in Hamburg, then exported that image back to England. The first time their manager-to-be Brian Epstein saw them on 9 November 1961 at the Cavern Club in Liverpool, he was simultaneously repulsed and enthralled. "It was a smoky, smelly, pretty squalid cellar and their act was ragged, undisciplined, and their clothes were a mess," described Brian. "Yet I recognized the appeal of their beat, and I rather liked their humor. I sensed something big – if it could be at once be harnessed and at the same time left untamed."[205]

Once he became their manager, Epstein deftly struck that balance between harnessed and untamed. By late 1963 and into early 1964, the Fab Four skyrocketed to worldwide fame and fortune due in part to their 'cleaned up' image. One fan wrote a letter to *The Washington Post*, published in the newspaper's 14 February 1964 issue, to that effect: "If the teen-agers of today would all follow the good examples set by The Beatles – not hair-wise, maybe, but certainly in the way of politeness, sense of humor and respect to others – tomorrow's generation would be greatly improved."[206] (Lennon later admitted it was just a veneer: "We had that image, but man, our tours were like something else … Just think

---

203 Beatles 2003, Episode 2
204 Norman, p. 91
205 *Time*, 8 September 1967, p. 54
206 *The Washington Post*, 14 February 1964, p. B13

of [Federico Fellini's prurient 1969 film] *Satyricon* with four musicians going through it."[207]) Thus, young listeners could join the Beatles bandwagon without being thought of as delinquents, and parents, though they often detested the band, were also more tolerant of their children listening to the Beatles than to the more intimidating Rock 'n' Rollers. As Epstein once put it:

> Their beat is something like Rock 'n' Roll but different from it. ... They have none of that mean hardness about them. They are genuine. They have life, humor, and strange, handsome looks. ... Mummies like the Beatles, too – that's the extraordinary thing. They think they are rather sweet. They approve.[208]

The same words don't apply to Elvis Presley, Little Richard, or the like.

The approval accorded the Beatles extended well beyond just 'Mummies'. The quartet's first American press conference occurred shortly after their arrival at the recently renamed John F. Kennedy airport in New York City on 7 February 1964. Their trademark quick wit and humor was on full display.

QUESTION: Are those English accents?

GEORGE: It's not English. It's Liverpudlian, you see.

QUESTION: Liverpool is the –

RINGO: [joking] It's the capital of Ireland.

PAUL: Anyway, we wrote half of your folk songs in Liverpool.

QUESTION: In Detroit Michigan, they're handing out car stickers saying, 'Stamp Out The Beatles.'

PAUL: Yeah well, first of all, we're bringing out a Stamp Out Detroit campaign.

QUESTION: There's some doubt that you can sing.

JOHN: No, we need money first.

QUESTION: How many of you are bald, that you have to wear those wigs?

JOHN: Oh, we're all bald, yeah. And deaf and dumb, too.

PAUL: Don't tell anyone, please.

QUESTION: Aren't you afraid of what the American Barbers Association is going to think of you?

---

207 Wenner, p. 61
208 *The New Yorker*, 28 December 1963, p. 23-24

RINGO: Well, we run quicker than the English ones, we'll have a go here.

QUESTION: Are you going to get a haircut at all while you're here?

BEATLES: No!

GEORGE: I had one yesterday.

RINGO: You should have seen him the day before.

QUESTION: What do you think of Beethoven?

RINGO: Great. Especially his poems.[209]

The Beatles were well-practiced at this type of banter with the press – they had been giving practically identical interviews in England for the last year – but America had never seen or heard anything like it. Only after the fact did the reporters who covered the event admit that they were not sent to promote the band but rather diminish their stature. "I watched amazed," said the Beatles' photographer Dezo Hoffman, "as 200 hard-boiled reporters who'd come to destroy the Beatles ended up adoring them."[210] The Beatles charmed the American media, and, because of the technology available to those media, in turn charmed the nation. "Great Britain hasn't been as influential in American affairs since 1775," opened an article in the 15 February 1964 issue of *Billboard*.[211] The same magazine featured the headlines "Beatle Binge In Los Angeles", "Chicago Flips Wig; Beatles And Otherwise", "New York City Crawling With Beatlemania", and "LBJ Ignored As N.Y. Crowds Chase Beatles".[212]

## Sights and Sounds

The Beatles' famous Liverpudlian accents also contributed to their mass appeal. "When the Beatles spoke with their thick Scouse accents, British listeners immediately detected the regional dialect and thought of downtrodden Liverpool," observes Steven D. Stark. "Americans, on the other hand, were unschooled in the intricacies of UK regional dialects and thought all Englishmen sounded the same. Thus they couldn't help but associate the Beatles with suave British actors such as Sir Laurence Olivier and David Niven."[213]

---

209  http://www.beatlesinterviews.org/db1964.0207.beatles.html, accessed 3 April 2015
210  Stark, p. 19
211  *Billboard*, 15 February 1964, p. 4
212  *Billboard*, 15 February 1964, p. 1, 8
213  Stark, p. 20

The band's innovative musical and spoken sounds would have commanded attention by themselves, but that combined with their equally startling appearance to catapult to foursome to even greater notoriety.

Masculinity in 1950s America emphasized strength, toughness, and muscular physiques. The predominant men's hair style was a sharply defined military crew cut. With their shaggy hair, round faces, and androgynous appearance, the Beatles provided a stark counter to the era's hyper-masculine epitome. "Teen-agers who once considered the G.I. crew-cut the height of adolescent fashion are letting their locks curl down their necks and over ears and across foreheads," observed Paul Gardner in the 9 February 1964 *New York Times.*[214] The fact that female fans responded so enthusiastically to what Leonard calls "a new model of masculinity,"[215] meant that young men across the nation would accept it as well.

Furthermore, the Beatles' unusual hairstyle offered young people a chance to imitate – no musical purchase or prowess necessary – making it an ideal way for fans to express allegiance to their brand of rebellious charm. The 25 January 1964 issue of *Billboard* advertised:

> If you're Beatle-minded, you can have your hair cut and a record, all in one clip. New Street Music, a record shop here located next door to a barber shop, will send you next door for a free haircut if you buy a Capitol Beatle LP. If you get a Beatle cut at the barber shop, you'll get a free album.[216]

When asked about the band's tremendous success, Paul McCartney cited "the haircuts. We didn't think they were a gimmick, but everyone else said, 'Oh-ho, what a gimmick.'"[185]

Many of the older generation couldn't understand the frenzy over the Beatles' music and looks. "Beatles Arrive, Teen-Agers Shriek, Police Do Their Duty, and That's That" read one front page *Washington Post* headline.[217] "An occasional cultural purgative can have a beneficial effect," wrote *New York Times* journalist Jack Gould derisively.[21] "We can just dismiss the Beatles as much ado about nothing," claimed writer Bill Gold.[218] Others were more harsh in their diatribes. An anonymous article published in the 11 February 1964 *Washington Post* states that

---

214   *The New York Times*, 9 February 1964 p. X19
215   Leonard, p. 195
216   *Billboard*, 25 January 1964, p. 1
217   *The Washington Post*, 12 February 1964, p. A1
218   *The Washington Post*, 10 February 1964, p. B22

"the mop-like appendage on the Beatle skull produces a look of amiable idiocy".[183] In the same newspaper's next issue, columnist Lawrecen Laurent's article, headlined "Beatles Set Back Cultural Exchange", describes the band as "hillbillies who look like sheep dogs and sound like alley cats in agony."[219]

Parents and teachers felt the Beatles' effect vicariously. "Reports of confrontations between teachers and long-haired students appear almost weekly in the newspapers," reports Gloria Emerson in the 23 July 1964 *New York Times*. "Students have been threatened with suspension, forbidden to play in interschool athletics, scolded, forced to tie their hair back with ribbons, and, in several instances, made to submit to barbers."[220]

Film director Robert Zemeckis' 1978 movie *I Wanna Hold Your Hand*, a fictional recreation of the mania that occurred in New York City during the Beatles' first U.S. visit, includes a scene in which a boy was 'made to submit to a barber' by his father. Another – this one real – was Bob Greene, who wrote in the 23 March entry of his memoir *Be True to Your School: A Diary of 1964*, "Dad told me to get a haircut; that kills me. So I did; I got it all cut off. It looks horrible. I swear, this is the last time I'm doing it. ... We ran into some girls on Main Street and tried to be cool for them, but they wanted nothing to do with us. I think it was probably because my haircut is so creepy."[221]

One couple discovered an amusing way to counter their children's enthusiasm: "Our kids [a 16-year-old son and a 15-year-old daughter] were the biggest Beatle fans on the block," explained the father. "They were driving us insane. We tried everything. We threatened them, we tried to bribe them, we begged them, to no avail. Then Alice got a brainstorm. If we went for the Beatles in a big way, they would have to stop liking them. So Alice bought a record and I got a Beatle hairdo and now the kids are completely off the Beatles."[222]

### A Hard Day's Night

The cultural success the Beatles established in the early months of 1964 accelerated as the year went on. The band's first movie, *A Hard Day's Night* (premiered 6 July 1964[223]), emphasized and extended their

219  *The Washington Post*, 12 February 1964, p. C7
220  *The New York Times*, 23 July 1964, p. 29
221  Greene, p. 73
222  *The Washington Post*, 18 February 1964, p. B23
223  Miles, p. 153

associations with Youth Culture.

One way the Beatles accentuated their youth on film was by hiring an actor substantially older than they were. Wilfrid Brambell was a few weeks shy of his 53$^{rd}$ birthday when filming began. Brambell plays the role of Paul McCartney's fictitious and unnamed grandfather. Though he's cantankerous and constantly getting into mischief (for that matter, so are all four Beatles), he is the only character in the film older than the band who is not portrayed negatively. Every other adult character is portrayed as the enemy – the antithesis of fun and youth.

John, Paul, George, and Ringo are ostensibly led by Norm and Shake, who function as their managers. The pair direct the band on what to do, where to go, how to act, et cetera. But in reality, the four musicians give their supposed superiors more headaches than respect. In the opening train scene, Norm pleads with the Beatles to behave themselves:

> NORM: Now, listen. I've had a marvelous idea. Just for a change, let's all behave like ordinary responsible citizens. Let's not cause any trouble, pull any strokes or do anything I'm going to be sorry for, especially tomorrow at the television theater because – Are you listening to me, Lennon?
>
> JOHN: You're a swine.

Even before the initial scene, Norm is shown as incompetent. While the Beatles are chased by adoring fans, Norm purchases milk from a vending machine, struggles to get the package open, and ultimately tears it, spilling milk all over himself. Norm adds nothing to the scene other than to show from the very beginning of the film that he's a fool.

In contrast to the stressed-out Norm, Shake is portrayed as happy-go-lucky and dim-witted. Together, they make a bumbling duo – a 1960s Tweedledee and Tweedledum – with Norm constantly complaining that Shake is taller than he is, and Shake explaining that he can't help it. Neither man has any true jurisdiction over the Beatles.

Later in the film, as Norm's micro-managing continues to suffocate the band, the foursome escapes through a fire exit and runs around outside as a way to blow off steam. But the relief is short-lived, and all too soon they are interrupted by a cranky older man. "I suppose you realize this is private property," he scolds, putting an abrupt end to their reverie. "Sorry we hurt your field, Mister," George responds sarcastically as they walk away.

Like Norm, the unnamed television producer (played by Victor

Spinetti) is also an authority figure lacking any authority. The Beatles are a constant burden for him, relentless in their verbal attacks. One scene in particular captures this atmosphere:

> DIRECTOR: If they aren't on this floor in 30 seconds there'll be trouble. Understand me? Trouble.
>
> [A moment later, the Beatles walk in.]
>
> JOHN: (to the director) Standing about, eh? Some people have it dead easy.
>
> DIRECTOR: [repressing frustration] Once you're over 30, you're past it. It's a young man's medium and I just can't stand the pace.
>
> RINGO: Oh, as young as that, then?
>
> DIRECTOR. I was. [He storms off with his secretary right behind him.]
>
> JOHN: Ah, there he goes. Look at him. I bet his wife doesn't know about her. I bet he hasn't even got a wife. Look at his sweater.
>
> PAUL: You never know, she might have knitted it.
>
> JOHN: She knitted him.

Another example of older people portrayed negatively is the scene in which the four Beatles share a train car with a middle-aged man. As soon as the man enters, there is confusion as he gets tangled up with Shake, Norm, and Grandfather. Once seated, he looks disdainfully at each of the Beatles. They proceed to argue over whether the window should be open or closed. When Ringo turns on a portable radio, the man reacts immediately:

> MAN : And we'll have that thing off as well, thank you.
>
> RINGO: But I –
>
> MAN: An elementary knowledge of the Railway Acts would tell you I'm perfectly within my rights.
>
> PAUL: Yeah, but we want to hear it and there's more of us than you. ...
>
> JOHN: Knock it off, Paul. You can't win with his sort. After all, it's his train, isn't it, Mister?
>
> MAN: Don't you take that tone with me, young man. I fought the war for your sort.
>
> RINGO: I bet you're sorry you won!

In contrast with those senior moments, young people are portrayed favorably. When Ringo goes out parading, he briefly befriends a boy named Charlie.

RINGO: How old are you anyway?

CHARLIE: Eleven.

RINGO: I bet you're only ten and a half.

CHARLIE: Ten and two thirds. ...

RINGO: Why aren't you at school?

CHARLIE: I'm a deserter.

RINGO: Are you now?

CHARLIE: Yeah, I've blown school out. ... Why aren't you at work?

RINGO: I'm a deserter, too.

By establishing that both of them are deserters, Ringo (and viewers along with him) connects to young Charlie through mutual experience and understanding in a way that he can't with anybody older.

*   *   *   *   *   *   *   *   *

*A Hard Day's Night* culminated the Beatles' Teenybopper phase. As they matured as people and artists, their music assumed progressively more adult themes. In the opening lyrics of their 1965 track 'Help!', John Lennon sings, "When I was young, so much younger than today", showing right from the start that the Beatles are acting significantly older, even though it's just one year later. The same year, Paul McCartney would sing nostalgically about believing in 'Yesterday', a song which similarly shifts from an energetic, youthful perspective to a more mature, wistful perspective.

A year after that, the band stopped touring, putting an end to one era in Fab Four history and initiating another. They would continue to lead Youth Culture, but from then on it would be designated by the term 'Counterculture' for its pronounced opposition to all things mainstream.

# CONCLUSION

## The Passing of the Torch

The sudden onset of Beatlemania in America cannot be attributed to any single event, person, or group of people. Instead, it was a combination of promotional effort with a string of historical coincidences:

- The Baby Boom and the consequent rise of Youth Culture

As a result of the post-WWII Baby Boom and the economic stability of the 1950s, there were simply more young people in America than ever before, and those young people had plentiful spending money. That, combined with the strong need for mid-20th Century youth to break from previous generations, yielded a pronounced rise in Youth Culture which had innovative aesthetic values.

- Brian Epstein's management

"The Beatle phenomenon is bound to set historians searching for the precise thing that triggered it," speculated the authors of *Life* magazine in their 28 August 1964 issue. "They need look no further than the simple intuition of a bland and exceedingly improbable young British businessman named Brian Epstein."[224] While this statement might be an oversimplification, it is not far from the truth.

Just as Kennedy knew the value of image, so too did Brian Epstein. He took the aggressive, dirty, and unrefined early Beatles and polished their image into clean and handsome, albeit strange-looking, young men. It was a savvy political move – one worthy of John Kennedy – because that image lead to a greater degree of acceptability and mass appeal.

---

224  *Life*, 28 August 1964, p. 62

Epstein was also responsible for booking their performances, including the all-important Ed Sullivan Show. Without those appearances
and accompanying broadcasts to serve as defining moments of Beatlemania in America, and without Epstein's general marketing insight and
indefatigable promotional efforts, Beatlemania could easily have stalled.

- Capitol's release of Beatles records

Since both Vee Jay and Swan Records had released unsuccessful
Beatles singles in the United States in early- to mid-1963, the fall of that
year was 'now or never' for the Beatles in America. With each failed release, the odds of the band's success in the New World decreased.

But neither Vee Jay nor Swan had the resources or political clout
within the industry to garner the attention that a major label such as
Capitol could. When Capitol finally decided to give the Beatles a try, the
label's stature gave the Beatles' music a respect the two other labels could
not provide. Since Capitol found the band worthy of release, the logic
went, perhaps the Beatles were worth another listen.

- Capitol's $40,000 promotional budget

Brian Epstein knew that any further American releases would
need promotional support to succeed. That's why he insisted on a
$40,000 advertising budget for further Beatle releases in the U.S. (see
page 3). Fortunately, Capitol's president Alan Livingston agreed.

- Media coverage

Since the phenomenon of musicians inspiring mass hysteria
dates back well before the Beatles (see page 47), it is clear that more than
just music was responsible for inducing Beatlemania and catapulting it to
unprecedented heights. A major contributing factor was the media coverage. The band's music, their famous wit and banter, and their cutting
edge looks all combined to charm both English and American reporters
and photographers. Through those media, the Beatles were able to charm
vast audiences, creating what Candy Leonard calls "a three-way relationship ... between the fans, the Beatles, and the media."[225]

- Technological advancements

Television widely disseminated the hysteria of Beatlemania on

---

225 Leonard, p. 20

both sides of the Atlantic. It allowed the Beatles' landmark Ed Sullivan Show performance on 9 February 1964 to be seen by 73.7 million viewers across the country.

Television also replaced radio as the primary communications medium over the course of the 1950s, thus freeing radio from broadcasting news events and forcing it to assume more of an entertainment character. This meant radio played more music in general and Beatles songs in particular. The band capitalized on both the new medium of television and the consequent new role of radio.

- Kennedy's assassination

John F. Kennedy's life and death primed the United States of America for the arrival of the Beatles. He was enthusiastic and dynamic, ushering in a fresh, energetic era of American society. Much of the country was accepting that change when he died, and was ready to welcome the Beatles, who had those same qualities. As Leonard observes, Kennedy "sought to harness the power of youth to promote positive social change on a global scale – the same youth power the Beatles would tap into in a few short years."[226]

As one biographer's title proclaims, Kennedy lived "an unfinished life".[227] This left an open-ended legacy. "With his death," wrote Martha Wolfenstein and Gilbert Kliman in *Children and the Death of a President*, "and particularly a death that resembles martyrdom, he not only becomes still more idealized, but there is a strong tendency to want to perpetuate him."[228] An article in the 29 November 1963 issue of *The Spectator* suggests "what perhaps endeared President Kennedy to the world more than his predecessors in office was the feeling that he represented the future. The only way in which we can pay tribute to him is by keeping a certain ideal of the future alive within ourselves."[229]

Bereavement counselors Claude L. Normand, Phyllis R. Silverman, and Steven L. Nickman observed that children often "showed signs of having internalized the deceased's values, goals, personalities, or behaviors as a way of remaining connected to the forever absent" in what the authors describe as a "living legacy".[230] Furthermore, the phenomenon is not always intentional. "Seeing themselves as a living legacy was not al-

---

226  Leonard, p. 3
227  Dallek 2003
228  Wolfenstein, p. 206
229  *The Spectator*, 29 November 1963, p. 681
230  Klass, Silverman, and Nickman, p. 93

ways a conscious choice," the authors continue, "it was something that happened."[231]   Thus, American adolescents' emphatic embrace of the Beatles in early 1964 can be at least partially attributed to the (not necessarily conscious) desire to continue Kennedy's legacy.

Kennedy dreamed of a cavalcade of leaders, societies, and cultures featuring new, youthful participants, but could not have anticipated how the Beatles would be the marshals of that parade. And the Beatles certainly did not intend to capitalize on his death. Nevertheless, that is precisely what happened. Since both JFK and the Beatles symbolized Youth Culture, when the former died, the latter took his place as a leader of Youth Culture. The sudden loss on 22 November 1963 of the man who epitomized the New Frontier left a gaping hole in the nation's collective consciousness and well-being. For the burgeoning American Youth Culture of the 1960s, the Beatles filled that hole by fulfilling the progressive promises of the fallen president.

*   *   *   *   *   *   *   *

John F. Kennedy symbolized change at a time when America was changing dramatically. Because of his untimely death, he never saw the culmination of the innovations he envisioned. Instead, the Beatles picked up where Kennedy left off, channeling his youth-centric philosophy into unprecedented worldwide cultural revolution.

Thus, while the notion that 'Kennedy made America sad, then the Beatles made America happy' is more or less accurate, this simplistic suggestion does not take into account the "shift in consciousness that occurred in those brief thousand days"[232] of the Kennedy era, nor does it recognize the strong parallels between the president and the band that allowed this transfer to happen in the first place – their connection runs much deeper.

Every revolution requires an enemy – a person, group, or object to overthrow. In the case of the Youth Culture revolution of the 1960s, that enemy was age and the complacency that goes with it. "The old ways will not do,"[233] said Kennedy, summarizing his entire philosophy in just six little words – and the same meaning underlies the phenomenon of Beatlemania.

---

231  Klass, Silverman, and Nickman, p. 94
232  Leonard, p. 18
233  *The New York Times*, 16 July 1960, p. 7

# Suggestions for Further Reading

There is no shortage of literature on either John F. Kennedy or the Beatles. In researching for this book, I read many (though hardly all) of the available texts on both. Below are recommendations for those seeking more information on one or the other. All of these sources proved extraordinarily helpful in my own research and understanding of the events discussed and analyzed in this book.


ON KENNEDY:


As Kennedy's official photographer, the late Jacques Lowe had personal insight into Kennedy's life. He published several books – among others, *Portrait: The Emergence of John F. Kennedy* (1961), *JFK Remembered* (1993), and *Remembering Jack: Intimate and Unseen Photographs of the Kennedys* (2003) – in which he drew on that experience, providing unique insights and first-hand accounts of Kennedy's career.

Although there seems to be little originality in Bill O'Reilly and Martin Dugard's *Killing Kennedy: The End of Camelot*, the book was the first I read and it inspired me to read more. The book is ideal for anyone seeking a place to start learning about Kennedy.

Another ideal starting point is PBS's American Experience documentary *JFK: Like No Other*. As of January 2015, it was available on Netflix. It was while watching that film that the idea behind this book first occurred to me.

Historian Robert Dallek's 2003 book *An Unfinished Life: John F. Kennedy 1917-1963* and 2013 book *Camelot's Court: Inside the Kennedy White House* are both exceptionally well-researched and documented, and provide excellent objective analysis of both Kennedy's strengths and weaknesses.

In terms of a primary source from the period on the effects of Kennedy's assassination on the youth of the time, there's no better book than Martha Wolfenstein and Gilbert Kliman's *Children and the Death of a President*.

Lastly, *The New York Times* extensively chronicled the 1960 presidential campaigns. There is no better primary source – including complete transcripts of many of Kennedy's speeches, conferences, and debates. The newspaper also documents on a day-by-day basis where Kennedy was campaigning and the responses he received, all of which are invaluable to a researcher.

## ON THE BEATLES:

Although he and I fundamentally disagree on the impact of Kennedy's assassination on American Beatlemania, Bruce Spizer is an excellent author. His impeccably researched and exceptionally well-written 2003 book *The Beatles Are Coming!: The Birth of Beatlemania in America* it is the definitive text on the subject and was invaluable as a resource for dates. The plentiful color photographs are also a treat!

While I wrote this book because I believe nobody else had yet exhausted the parallels between Kennedy and the Beatles, Jonathan Gould's *Can't Buy Me Love: The Beatles, Britain, and America* and Steven D. Stark's *Meet the Beatles: A Cultural History of the Band that Shook Youth, Gender, and the World* do discuss similarities. Though I believe neither provides the depth of historical context or draws conclusions to the extent that I have, both authors' insights helped shape my own research and writing. Similarly, Candy Leonard's *Beatleness: How the Beatles and their Fans Remade the World* does a wonderful job of putting the Beatles' arrival in America into historical context by explaining the historical climate and political atmosphere of America during Kennedy's presidency.

Lastly, though his work doesn't directly relate to this book directly, it's impossible to overestimate the impact of Mark Lewisohn's contributions to Beatles scholarship. His books *The Beatles Recording Sessions*, *The Complete Beatles Chronicle*, and *The Beatles: All These Years, Volume 1: Tune In* are the gold standard of Beatles books.

# References

Adler, Bill, Ed. 1964. *The Kennedy Wit*. The Citadel Press; New York, NY.

Adler, Bill. 1965. *John F. Kennedy and the Young People of America*. David McKay Company, Inc.; New York, NY.

Andersen, Christopher. 1996. *Jack and Jackie: Portrait of an American Marriage*. William Morrow and Company, Inc.; New York, NY.

Ariès, Philippe. 1962. *Centuries of Childhood: A Social History of Family Life*. Trans. Robert Baldick. Alfred A. Knopf; New York, NY.

Barnouw, Erik. 1990. *Tube of Plenty: The Evolution of American Television*. Oxford University Press; New York, NY.

Beatles, The. 2000. *The Beatles Anthology*. Chronicle Books; San Francisco, CA.

- - - . 2003. *The Beatles Anthology*. Dir. Bob Smeaton, Geoff Wonfor, and Kevin Godley, DVD, Capitol.

- - - . no date. *A Hard Day's Night*. Dir. Richard Lester, DVD, Buena Vista Entertainment, Inc.

Blaney, John. 2005. *John Lennon: Listen To This Book*. Paper Jukebox, Biddles Ltd; Guildford, UK.

Brake, Michael. 1985. *Comparative Youth Culture: The Sociology of Youth Culture and Youth Sub-Cultures in America, Britain and Canada*. Routledge & Kegan Paul; Boston, MA.

Brown, Peter and Steven Gaines. 1983. *The Love You Make: An Insider's Story of the Beatles*. McGraw-Hill Book Company; New York, NY.

Carlin, Peter Ames. 2009. *Paul McCartney: A Life*. A Touchstone Book, published by Simon & Schuster; New York, NY.

Carwardine, Richard. 2006. *Lincoln: A Life of Purpose and Power*. Alfred A. Knopf; New York, NY.

Coleman, James S. 1961. *The Adolescent Society: The Social Life of the Teenager and its Impact on Education*. The Free Press of Glencoe, a division of the Crowell-Collier Publishing Company; New York, NY.

Collis, John. 2002. *Chuck Berry: The Biography*. Aurum Press; London, UK.

Covach, John. 2009. *What's That Sound?: An Introduction to Rock and Its History*. Second edition. W. W. Norton & Company; New York, NY.

Dallek, Richard. 2003. *An Unfinished Life: John F. Kennedy 1917-1963*. Little, Brown, and Company; Boston, MA.

- - - . 2013. *Camelot's Court: Inside the Kennedy White House*. HarperCollins Publishers; New York, NY.

Duvall, Evelyn Millis. 1947. *Keeping Up With Teen-Agers*. The Public Affairs Committee, Incorporated.

Epstein, Brian. *A Cellarful of Noise*. Pyramid Books; New York, NY.

Evans, Mike. 2002. *Elvis: A Celebration*. A DK Publishing Book; New York, NY.

Fasick, Frank A. 1984. "Parents, Peers, Youth Culture and Autonomy in Adolescence" in *Adolescence*, Spring 1984, pages 19, 73.

Fitzgerald, Helen. 2000. *The Grieving Teen: A Guide for Teenagers and Their Friends*. A Fireside Book, published by Simon & Schuster; New York, NY.

Foner, Eric and John A. Garraty, ed. 1991. *The Reader's Companion to American History*. Houghton Mifflin Company; Boston, MA.

Forest, Tennant. 2012. "John F. Kennedy's Pain Story: From Autoimmune Disease to Centralized Pain" in *Practical Pain Management*, September 2012, pages 53-68.

Freedman, Eric and Edward Hoffman. 2005. Citadel Press, Kensington Publishing Corp.; New York, NY.

Fryd, Hallie. 2012. *Scandalous!: 50 Shocking Events You Should Know About (So You Can Impress Your Friends)*. Zest Books; San Francisco, CA.

Geller, Debbie. Edited by Anthony Wall. 2000. *In My Life: The Brian Epstein Story*. Thomas Dunne Books, an imprint of St. Martin's Press; New York, NY.

Goldsmith, Martin. 2004. *The Beatles Come to America*. John Wiley & Sons, Inc.; Hoboken, NJ.

Gould, Jonathan. *Can't Buy Me Love: The Beatles, Britain, and America*.

Harmony Books; New York, NY, 2007.

Greene, Bob. 1987. *Be True to Your School: A Diary of 1964*. Ballantine Books; New York, NY.

Guralnick, Peter. 1994. *Last Train to Memphis: The Rise of Elvis Presley*. Little, Brown and Company; Boston, MA.

*Hard Day's Night, A.* Richard Lester dir., Miramax Films, distributed by Buena Vista Home Entertainment, no date.

Hellmann, John. 1997. *The Kennedy Obsession: The American Myth of JFK*. Columbia University Press; New York, NY.

Hersh, Seymour M. 1997. *The Dark Side of Camelot*. Little, Brown and Company; Boston, MA.

Hindman, Hugh D. 2002. *Child Labor: An American History*. M.E. Sharpe; Armonk, NY.

Hobbs, Sandy, Jim McKechnie and Michael Lavalette. 1999. *Child Labor: A World History Companion*. ABC-CLIO; Denver, CO.

Hoxie, Paul and David Skinner. 1988. *A Statistical Analysis of the Effects of a Uniform Minimum Drinking Age*. US Department of Transportation, National Highway Traffic Safety Administration; Washington D.C.

Jackson, John Wyse. 2005. *We All Want to Change the World: The Life of John Lennon*. Hause Books; London, UK.

Jeffers, H. Paul. 2000. *An Honest President: The Life and Presidencies of Grover Cleveland*. William Morrow, an imprint of HarperCollins Publishers; New York, NY.

Kandel, Denise B. and Gerald S. Lesser. 1972. *Youth in Two Worlds*. Jossey-Bass Inc., Publishers; San Francisco, CA.

Klass, Dennis, Phullis R. Silverman, and Steven L. Nickman, ed. 1996. *Continuing Bonds: New Understandings of Grief*. Taylor & Francis; Washington DC.

Kozinn, Allan. 1995. *The Beatles*. Phaidon Press; London, UK.

Laing, Dave. 2010. *Buddy Holly.* Indiana University Press; Bloomington, IN.

Leigh, Spencer. 2013. *The Beatles in America: The Stories, The Scene, 50 Years On*. Metro Books; New York, NY.

Leonard, Candy. 2014. *Beatleness: How the Beatles and their Fans Remade the World.* Arcade Publishing; New York, NY.

Lewisohn, Mark. 1988. *The Beatles Recording Sessions.* Harmony Books; New York, NY.

- - - . 2006. *The Complete Beatles Chronicle.* Hamlyn, an imprint of Octopus Publishing Group Limited; London, UK.

- - - . 2013. *The Beatles: All These Years, Volume 1: Tune In.* Crown Archetype, an imprint of the Crown Publishing Group, a division of Random House LLC, a Penguin Random House Company; New York, NY.

Lowe, Jacques. 1961. *Portrait: The Emergence of John F. Kennedy.* Bramhall House; New York, NY.

- - - . 1993. *JFK Remembered.* Random House; New York, NY.

- - - . 2003. *Remembering Jack: Intimate and Unseen Photographs of the Kennedys.* A Bob Adelman Book, Bulfinch Press, AOL Time Warner Book Group; Boston, MA.

Martin, George. 1994. *With a Little Help From My Friends: The Making of Sgt. Pepper.* Little, Brown and Company; Boston, MA.

Martland, Peter. 1997. *Since Records Began: EMI the First 100 Years.* Amadeus Press; Portland, OR.

Matthews, Christopher. 1996. *Kennedy & Nixon: The Rivalry that Shaped Postwar America.* Simon & Schuster; New York, NY.

- - - . 2011. *Jack Kennedy: Elusive Hero.* Simon & Schuster; New York, NY.

MacDonald, Ian. 1994. *Revolution in the Head: The Beatles' Records and the Sixties.* Henry Holt and Company; New York, NY.

MacDonald, J. Fred. 1985. *Television and the Red Menace: The Video Road to Vietnam.* Praeger; New York, NY.

- - - . 1999. *One Nation Under Television: The Rise and Decline of Newtork TV.* Nelson-Hall Publishers; Chicago, IL.

Manchester, William. 1967. *The Death of a President: November 20 - November 25, 1963.* Harper & Row; New York, NY.

Maynard, Joyce. 1973. *Looking Back: A Chronicle of Growing Up Old in the Sixties.* Doubleday & Company, Inc.; Garden City, NY.

Meisler, Stanley. 2011. *When the World calls" The Inside Story of the Peace Corps and its First Fifty Years.* Beacon Press; Boston, MA.

Miles, Barry. 2001. *The Beatles Diary, Volume 1: The Beatle Years.* Omnibus Press; New York, NY.

Mintz, Steven and Susan Kellogg. 1988. *Domestic Revolutions: A Social History of American Family Life*. The Free Press, a division of Macmillan, Inc.; New York, NY.

Murray, Michael D. ed. 1999. *Encyclopedia of Television News*. Oryx Press; Phoenix, AZ.

Norman, Philip. 1996. *Shout!: The Beatles in their Generation*. A Fireside Book, published by Simon & Schuster; New York, NY.

- - - . 2008. *John Lennon: The Life*. ECCO, an imprint of HarperCollins; New York, NY.

O'Reilly, Bill and Martin Dugard. 2012. *Killing Kennedy: The End of Camelot*. Henry Holt and Company, LLC; New York, NY.

Pawlowski, Gareth. 1989. *How They Became the Beatles: A Definitive History of the Early Years: 1960-1964*. E. P. Dutton; New York, NY.

Pietrusza, David. 2008. *1960, LBJ vs. JFK vs. Nixon: The Epic Campaign That Forged Three Presidencies*. Union Square Press, an imprint of Sterling Publishing Co., Inc.; New York, NY.

Reeves, Richard. 1993. *President Kennedy: Profile of Power*. A Touchstone Book, Published by Simon & Schuster; New York, NY.

Riley, Tim. 2011. *Lennon: The Man, the Myth, the Music – The Definitive Life*. Hyperion; New York, NY.

Sabata, Larry J. 2013. *The Kennedy Half-Century: The Presidency, Assassination, and Lasting Legacy of John F. Kennedy*. Bloomsbury; New York, NY.

Sanders, Catherine. 1989. *Grief: The Mourning After*. A Wiley-Interscience Publication, John Wiley & Sons; New York, NY.

Schaffner, Nicholas. 1977. *The Beatles Forever*. Cameron House, an imprint of Stackpole Books; Harrisburg, PA.

Schlesinger Jr., Arthur M. 1965. *A Thousand Days: John F. Kennedy in the White House*. Houghton Mifflin Company, Boston, MA.

Shotton, Pete and Nicholas Schaffner. 1984. *The Beatles, Lennon, and Me*. Stein and Day; New York, NY.

Sinatra, Nancy. 1995. *Frank Sinatra: An American Legend*. General Publishing Group, Inc.; Santa Monica, CA.

Spizer, Bruce. 2003. *The Beatles Are Coming!: The Birth of Beatlemania in America*. 498 Productions, L.L.C.; New Orleans, LA.

Steinberg, Laurence. 2008. *Adolescence*. McGraw Hill; Boston, MA.

Stokes, Geoffrey. 1980. *The Beatles*. Times Books, a Rolling Stone Press Book; New York, NY.

Sounes, Howard. 2010. *Fab: An Intimate Life of Paul McCartney*. Da Capo Press, A Member of the Perseus Books Group; Philadelphia, PA.

Stark, Steven D. 2005. *Meet the Beatles: A Cultural History of the Band that Shook Youth, Gender, and the World*. HarperCollins; New York, NY.

Trattner, Walter I. 1970. *Crusade for Children: A History of the National Child Labor Committee and Child Labor Reform in America*. Quadrangle Books; Chicago, IL.

Troy, Gil. *See How They Ran: The Changing Role of the Presidential Candidate*. The Free Press, a division of MacMillan, Inc.; New York, NY.

Trynka, Paul, editor in chief. 2004. *The Beatles: Ten Years that Shook the World*. Dorling Kindersley Limited; London, UK.

Walker, Alan. 1983. *Franz Liszt, volume 1: The Virtuoso Years, 1811-1847*. Knopf, distributed by Random House; New York, NY.

Wayne, Tiffany K, ed. 2015. *Women's Rights in the United States: A Comprehensive Encyclopedia of Issues, Events, and People, Volume 1*. ABC-CLIO, LLC; Santa Barbara, CA.

Wenner, Jan. 2000. *Lennon Remembers*. Verso; New York, NY.

Whitburn, Joel. 2004. *The Billboard Book of Top 40 Hits*. Billboard Books, an imprint of Watson-Guptill Publications; New York, NY.

White, Charles. 1994. *The life and times of Little Richard: The Quasar of Rock*. Harmony Books; New York, NY.

White, Theodore H. 1962. *The Making of the President 1960*. Giant Cardinal, by arrangement with Atheneum House, Inc.; New York, NY.

Wingenbach, Charles E. 1961. *The Peace Corps – Who, How, and Where*. The John Day Company; New York, NY.

Wolfenstein, Martha and Gilbert Kliman, ed. 1965. *Children and the Death of a President*. Doubleday & Company, Inc.; Garden City, NY.

Womack, Kenneth and Todd F. Davis. 2006. *Reading the Beatles: Cultural Studies, Literary Criticism, and the Fab Four*. State University of New York Press; Albany, NY.

# Index

# About the Author

America's only full-time professional Beatles scholar, Aaron Krerowicz won a research grant in November 2011 through the University of Hartford to study the band, and has since presented his findings through well more than one hundred presentations libraries, universities, continuing education programs, and community centers throughout the United States.

For his latest news, book releases, and presentation schedule, register for his free email newsletters, sent the 20th of each month, on his website: www.AaronKrerowicz.com.

\* \* \* \* \* \* \* \* \*

*From the Shadow of JFK* is Aaron's fourth book and third about the Beatles. He has several more planned for the coming years:

- *Let it Be: The Beatles, January 1969*, a look at the most tumultuous month of the Beatles' career and how those sessions yielded their last-released album.
- *Structural Analysis of Beatles Music*, an exhaustive study of how the Beatles structured their songs and how those structures developed over time.
- *Harmonic Analysis of Beatles Music*, a companion text to the above, a study of how the Beatles use chords and particular chord progressions.
- *Starr Time: A Celebration of Ringo Starr's Contributions to the Beatles*, showing how Ringo's personality, drumming, singing, and songwriting all aided in the band's success.